PRACTICING
CHRISTIAN
COMPASSION

# Practicing Christian Compassion

## 50 DEVOTIONS

### to Embody God's Grace in Your Daily Life

DALE AND TAMARA CHAMBERLAIN

**ROCKRIDGE
PRESS**

For general information on our other products and services or to obtain technical support, please contact our Customer Care Department within the United States at (866) 744-2665, or outside the United States at (510) 253-0500.

Rockridge Press publishes its books in a variety of electronic and print formats. Some content that appears in print may not be available in electronic books, and vice versa.

Interior and Cover Designer: Jami Spittler
Art Producer: Sue Bischofberger
Editors: Andrea Leptinsky and Carolyn Abate
Production Editor: Matt Burnett

All art used under license from Shutterstock.com
Author photograph courtesy of Hilary S. Barreto

ISBN: Print 978-1-64739-924-5 | eBook 978-1-64739-925-2
R0

To our son, Silas Chamberlain.
May you build a legacy of
compassion in your life
that reveals the heart of Jesus
to everyone you encounter.

# ⇌ Contents ⇌

# Introduction

Just about everyone thinks they're a compassionate person. Or at least they want to be. And yet, compassion isn't something that comes naturally to us—because it's hard. The Latin roots of the word *compassion* actually mean to "suffer with or alongside."

When you put it in those terms, it doesn't seem that pleasant. But compassion is based on the belief that when we are willing to suffer with and for one another, we will collectively suffer less. It seems counterintuitive, but it's a way of living that could change the world.

Wherever you are on your journey of compassion, you've taken a big step by picking up this book. You are committed to making a positive impact on the world and are looking for resources on how to do it.

Having a heart of compassion is more than just a trendy cultural movement or a way to become a better person. Its value is so much deeper than that. Jesus has built compassion into the eternal community of his people. But this isn't a culture that we'll need to wait until the other side of eternity to see. We can build a compassionate world here and now. The heart of Jesus has always been for his people to care for one another. He's inviting you to display his life-changing heart of compassion to others in everyday situations. It isn't always an easy calling, but it's one Jesus wants for all of his people.

We, Dale and Tamara, have dedicated our lives to being in ministry together. Over the years, we've served in churches, Christian camps, and other nonprofit organizations to see the mission of Jesus become reality. Ministry isn't easy work, and it comes with any number of challenges and heartaches. But we know that a willingness to endure difficulties is the calling of every Christian who wants to make an impact for good.

While we have always sought to teach compassion to others throughout our leadership and ministry, there are still moments that continue to teach us new ways to live compassionately.

For example, Dale served as one of the pastors at a church while it was going through a number of transitions in an effort to reach its community more effectively. In the midst of that, we both received a considerable amount of backlash from some members of the church. Nevertheless, we moved forward, fighting the "good fight." Our heart was to show the love of Jesus to the people in the community who didn't yet know him.

One weekend, we braced ourselves for yet another contentious congregational meeting. In that meeting, a number of church members stood up to share their frustrations with the church's leadership. The words of one woman in particular were especially piercing to our souls; they were not filled with grace or kindness, but anger and bitterness.

After the meeting, Tamara was filled with pain and despair, until she had found out more about the story of the woman who spoke at the meeting. As it turned out, the woman was going through a very traumatic situation in her life, and she was likely lashing out as a result of her own pain. It was at this moment that Tamara felt compassion for her; the words still stung, but the pain didn't cut as deep.

That was also the moment we realized that we had blind spots when it came to showing compassion to others—a moment we all experience. We hope this book will gently reveal some of your blind spots and nudge you toward becoming the most compassionate person you can be. The journey will have challenges, but humanizing and identifying with the pains and needs of others will empower us to love like Jesus does.

As your heart opens to being intentional about extending compassion, your eyes will open to your own shortcomings. But they will also open to the countless ways Jesus is moving in your life. You have such a beautiful opportunity to step into a greater sense of purpose, doing great work for the good of others and becoming everything that God has intended you to be.

# How to Use This Book

The hope of this book is that you will learn not only about compassion from a Christian perspective but also how to put it into action in your daily life. The book is divided into five sections, each of which focuses on helping you develop compassion in a particular part of your life: family, friends, colleagues and coworkers, local community, and global community. While each chapter is meant to explore compassion across many areas, starting at home and expanding globally, these sections need not necessarily be read in order. If you're particularly excited to grow in compassion in one of these areas, by all means, skip straight to that chapter.

Each devotional entry centers on a key Bible verse that expresses an important component of compassion. We'll spend some time exploring what the verse means as well as its practical implications for your personal compassion efforts. Each devotion also includes a prayer and a prompt. The prayer is intended to serve as a starting point for your conversation with God as you process the content of the day's devotion. While there's nothing magical about the words themselves, our hope is that they will orient your heart in response to what you have just read. The devotional prompts will then give you tangible steps to take toward living out different aspects of compassion. They are meant to be challenging and thought provoking. Acting on each prompt will be the most difficult part of learning compassion, because growing is hard. Learning *about* compassion is one thing, but this book is intended to help you apply compassion to your life.

Read this book at the pace that allows you to apply its truths as you go. However, if you read through it too quickly, you may find it difficult to adequately wrestle with everything you've learned and implement it into your life. We recommend taking things slowly, perhaps even focusing on applying what you've learned from as little as one devotional entry a week. On the other hand, if you'd like to gain a high-level understanding of the content, you are certainly welcome to do a quicker read of this book, returning to prompts that stand out to you most and that you would like to intentionally put into action.

In the Resources section (page 141), you will find charitable organizations and content creators that will help you further explore how you might implement compassion. These organizations range from educational sources meant to further your understanding to opportunities to actively participate in acts of compassion both at home and abroad.

As you dive into these devotionals, we pray that God will use them to build your understanding, expose any blind spots you may have, and inspire you to share your love and compassion in every setting and season of life.

## CHAPTER ONE

# FAMILY

**It has often been** said that "ministry starts at home." Before we're able to make an impact in the world, we need to bring positive change to the world inside the walls of our homes. This is a responsibility that we can too often overlook. So many of us have great visions for how to make the world a better place, but as we seek to make those dreams reality, our families can suffer.

As someone who has served in local church ministry for a long time, Dale has often felt this tension. Serving as a pastor, he has worked long and stressful hours because he believes what has often been said about the local church: It's the hope of the world. Jesus has chosen to work through the local church to bring about transformation within its community so that he can heal broken hearts, broken homes, broken systems, and broken lives.

But in an effort to give everything he has to that cause, Dale has, at times, forgotten to reserve some of his energy for his family. If you can identify with this struggle, then you probably know that this can make your family feel like they matter less to you than strangers. They may have even told you as much.

This is a difficult truth, but it's one we should sear into our minds. Even if you sacrifice all your time, resources, passion, and gifts for the cause of showing the world compassion, but you fail to love your family well, you have failed.

The people who are the closest to you are often the people who get the worst of you. You're quick to show compassion to people outside your home. You want to find ways to get involved. You want to come to the defense of the defenseless. You want to decrease suffering and increase joy in the world. All of these ambitions are pure and genuine, yet your family would never know it by the way you sometimes treat them.

Maybe the reason why we treat our families the worst—even though we care about them the most—is because they're so close to us that we see them as an extension of ourselves. But they aren't. Each of our family members is a unique person, toward whom we need to show empathy and compassion. We need to make the choice to see the world through their eyes so that we can learn how to love them better.

When you fail to show compassion to your family, it's not because you don't love them. It's because you haven't been as intentional about showing them compassion as you would the world.

Let's explore how to begin choosing intentional compassion for your family. When you allow Jesus to work through you to change your home, you'll be well on your way to changing the world.

# Compassion for the Suffering of Those Closest to You

*If you think you are too important to help someone, you are only fooling yourself. You are not that important.*

*Galatians 6:3, New Living Translation*

When someone in your home is experiencing a crisis, it almost never comes at a convenient time. Important matters outside the home are pressing, and you have a full schedule. You would never say it, but you feel like you don't have time for whatever it is your family member is dealing with right now.

But, as Paul writes to the church of Galatia, looking out for one another is a key aspect of our faith. Look out especially for those struggling with sin, he instructs, but be careful not to fall into temptation while you are helping. Above all, no one is above helping others in a time of need.

Maybe someone in your family is struggling right now. It could be an issue of active sin, a physical or mental illness, or a life transition. It's important that you be there for your family member during this time as best you can.

You need to be there for them when you don't understand, when you think their suffering isn't that significant, or when you can't relate. Suffering comes in many shapes and sizes. The best way to show compassion is to make the time to simply be there and listen.

Tamara's cousin had a horse that had recently passed away. Now, Tamara is not a fan of horses. In fact, she's afraid of them. So, she couldn't relate to the emotional pain her cousin experienced from the death of her horse.

But she could see her cousin's pain. Tamara knew that her cousin had received the horse as part of mourning her grandfather's death, and she understandably had a special bond with the animal. Though she couldn't make it go away, Tamara wanted to acknowledge and validate her cousin's pain. So, she sent a sympathy card as a small way to show compassion.

It can be the smallest gesture that lets someone who's suffering know that you're there for them.

### Prayer

*Father, I want to take a moment to open my eyes and heart to those suffering around me. Would you make me more aware and attentive to those suffering in my family? I want to extend compassion and love to them as you have called me to. Amen.*

### Prompt

As you go through your day, be aware of anyone in your family who is struggling. It may seem minor, like nervousness about a new job, or significant, like waiting for test results for a severe illness. How can you show that family member that you see them and are there for them?

# Caring Enough to Share Your Faith with Your Family

*How, then, can they call on the one they have not believed in? And how can they believe in the one of whom they have not heard? And how can they hear without someone preaching to them?*

Romans 10:14, New International Version

For some people, sharing their faith comes naturally. Dale has a friend who's unafraid to approach a stranger on the street and share a message of hope. Within minutes, this friend can be praying with them, encouraging them, and urging them to find their purpose in Jesus. And the people he approaches are always so responsive.

Dale doesn't have that gift. He has often struggled to find the right words to say in the right moments to help someone put their trust in Jesus. But he knows how important it is. As Paul says in his letter to the Romans, no one is able to experience the transformation that Jesus wants to bring to their life unless they put their faith in him. But they can't put their faith in Jesus unless someone tells them about him.

In order to grow in this area of his faith, Dale has spent a lot of time on college campuses, starting conversations with students and sharing the message of Jesus. And it has gotten easier. But there's one situation in which it never feels easy to share his faith: when he's speaking to his family.

Why is that the case for so many of us? Maybe it's because you've known your family members for so long that you don't feel confident that they're ever going to change. Maybe it's because they know you so well and can call out all your shortcomings and hypocrisies. Maybe the reason it's easier to talk to a stranger about Jesus is because there isn't any emotional baggage and you don't feel any danger of consequences to that relationship.

But of all the compassionate things you can do for a family member, you can't give them eternal meaning, purpose, and life. Only Jesus can do that. That said, you do have the unique ability and calling to invite them to experience the life-changing grace that you yourself have received.

## Prayer

*Father God, give me a sense of urgency when sharing my faith with my family. May I not be afraid of the consequences, and may I only be motivated by love. Use me to bring about life transformation to those I love most. Give me the words. Work through me. Amen.*

## Prompt

Begin praying for someone in your family who needs the hope of Jesus. Pray for them daily. Pray for their heart. Pray for *your* heart. Pray for opportunities to talk to them. Pray for the words to say. And then, mark out a time in your calendar where you want to sit down and speak with them about the hope you have and that you want them to have, too.

# Compassion for the Family Member You Disagree With

*If it is possible, as far as it depends on you, live at peace with everyone.*

Romans 12:18, New International Version

When you strongly disagree with someone on an important issue, it's all too easy to begin dehumanizing them, which is sure to cause more problems than it may seem to solve. Some of us are even guilty of doing it to the people in our own home.

Dale has certain family members who stand on the opposite side of him in almost every important issue of life, and it can be so frustrating and draining.

Maybe you've had a similar experience. You disagree with a family member politically, or maybe you just don't think that they're making good lifestyle choices. This can be especially difficult when your view contrasts so starkly with theirs and you both feel strongly about it.

But loving someone doesn't mean that you always have to agree with them. In his letter to the churches in Rome, Paul was addressing people who had upbringings, cultures, and political views that were profoundly different from one another. And yet, Paul called them to live at peace. We're called to do the same.

As much as it depends on you, live at peace with them. You don't need to convince yourself that their view is just as "right" as yours. It's okay to think they're wrong. But it's how you treat them as a person in spite of that disagreement that's important.

Do you regularly exercise empathy in relationships with family members you disagree with? Or are you cold with them? Do you give them the silent treatment or act passive-aggressively whenever a disagreement crops up? Do you withhold affection when they express an opinion that's different from yours?

You don't have control over how someone treats you because of your disagreement. Maybe they're guilty of doing all those things to you, too. In spite of that, as much as you can help it, seek to live at peace with that person. Try to at least understand their point of view, and actively choose to love them.

Peace is more than the absence of open conflict. It's the presence of love and compassion even despite genuine disagreement.

## Prayer

*God, help me grow in compassion for those in my family with whom I strongly disagree. Help me soften my approach toward them. Help me accept them as they are, just as you accept me as I am. Help me cultivate peace through compassion. Amen.*

## Prompt

The next time a deep disagreement flares up between you and a family member, take a moment to pause and let them know that you love them. Be genuine in telling them that you care for them even though you disagree with them. This will go a long way in rooting your interactions with them in love.

# Building Compassion Into Your Daily Conversations

*Therefore, as God's chosen people, holy and dearly loved, clothe yourselves with compassion, kindness, humility, gentleness, and patience.*

Colossians 3:12, New International Version

What you wear says a lot about who you are. It shows what you value, what you like, and how you want to be seen by the world. Like the physical clothing you put on, the intangible attributes you choose to adorn your life with also show a lot about who you are. That's why Paul calls us to clothe ourselves with compassion, kindness, humility, gentleness, and patience.

The problem is that most of us aren't very intentional about the kinds of attitudes and actions we "put on" when we wake up in the morning. When it comes to our hearts, we're like someone who thoughtlessly pulls the dirty, worn out, unfashionable clothing out of the hamper and puts those items on in the dark. One of the main ways you'll see the way your family members clothe their hearts is in how conversations naturally unfold in your home.

If you're anything like us, you probably speak very negatively about the people outside your home. Maybe it's with your spouse, your sibling, or your roommate. We certainly do this all the time. When we talk about our jobs, we spend a large part of our conversations picking apart the character flaws and idiosyncrasies of our coworkers. When we watch the news, we speak negatively about every news story we see.

We're quick to point out what annoys us but slow to see the world from other points of view.

In order for compassion to be a part of the *culture* of your household, it needs to constantly be a part of the *conversation* of your household. Your family's vocabulary needs to be compassionate, and that culture can begin with what your heart chooses to dwell on and the words you allow to pass through your lips.

## Prayer

*God, I'm sorry for the ways I have failed to cultivate compassionate conversation in my household. Help me lead my family into better habits when it comes to what we talk about and how we express our opinions. Help me develop more empathy and clothe myself in compassion every day. Amen.*

## Prompt

Within the next day or so, do a mental audit of the conversations you're having around your home or dinner table. How many of them are negative? How many of them involve speaking negatively about others? Have an honest conversation with your family about your desire to build a culture of compassionate conversation. Resolve to be gracious but to firmly hold one another accountable to this commitment.

# Compassion During Family Conflict

*A gentle answer turns away wrath, but a harsh word stirs up anger.*

Proverbs 15:1, New International Version

No one can hurt you quite like those who are closest to you. Their words pierce the deepest—their thoughtless actions wound us the worst—because they have greater access to the important things of your heart. The members of your family are the ones in your life who can bring you the most joy, but they can also bring you the most pain.

When you're in the middle of a conflict, you probably tend to dwell on all the ways that you've been hurt and treated unfairly. The unkind words spoken in anger toward you. And the most natural thing in the world is to move swiftly with a counterattack.

But as you seek to grow in compassion toward those closest to you, it's important to remember something: beneath every conflict is a hurt, and sometimes the cause of that hurt is you. The ancient wisdom of Proverbs tells us that when we respond with gentleness, we have the power to defuse conflict.

Rather than seeking to defend yourself or retaliating with an accusation of your own, try to understand the hurt beneath your loved one's words. Offer a gentle answer, even in response to an inflammatory remark.

Maybe there's something you need to apologize for. Maybe their misdirected anger toward you is coming from another situation in their life. Either way, seek to understand.

If you're able to do that, you'll find that conflict will begin to melt away. Mutual understanding will grow exponentially, and you will gain a bigger vision of the world by choosing to see it through the eyes of those you love most.

As you change the culture of conversation in your house, you will begin to promote compassion, empathy, and understanding. You can then begin to expand that world-changing culture beyond your home.

## Prayer

*God, grow my capacity to choose understanding over being understood. Give me eyes to see the hurts of my family and what part I've play in them. Help me let go of my desire to return every blow I receive. Help me be like Jesus in the midst of conflict with those closest to me. Amen.*

## Prompt

Think about the last conflict you had with a family member. What parts of that conflict can you own and take responsibility for? What do you need to apologize for? What was the hurt beneath the disagreement? Seek to understand the other person's perspective. If you haven't already, seek to reconcile that conflict, and let the other person know that you see and care for their hurts.

## COMPASSION BURNOUT TIP

As you attune your heart to the hurts of others, the weight and enormity of the needs you see can be overwhelming. As much as you're trying to make a difference, remember, you're only one person. It's easy to get discouraged or even experience feelings of apathy.

When you begin to feel compassion burnout, it's important to stop and remember one simple yet important truth: you are not the savior of the world. You never could be, and that's not what Jesus is asking you to do. He's just asking you to be faithful. So, be faithful and leave the world-saving to him.

# Bearing Financial Burdens
# with Your Family

*If anyone has material possessions and sees a brother
or sister in need but has no pity on them, how can the
love of God be in that person? Dear children, let us not
love with words or speech but with actions and in truth.*

1 John 3:17–18, New International Version

Money has a tendency to make things awkward. Throw complex family dynamics in the mix, and that's even more the case.

It's true that God cares about your spiritual well-being. But that's not all he cares about. He cares about the well-being of the whole person. So, as you seek to love others and show compassion to family members, be mindful of their whole self. Extending compassion is about more than listening to the needs of those in your family. It's also about seeing how you can care for their physical needs, even their financial ones. John tells us that our love for others is proof positive of the love God has placed within us.

Family dynamics are complicated. It's not as cut and dried as "see a need, fill a need." You certainly need to exercise wisdom and discernment as you seek to bear financial burdens with your family. With that in mind, it's important to understand that compassion in action isn't always comfortable. It requires sacrifices in areas you might not want to sacrifice.

Tamara grew up with a single mom who struggled to make ends meet. There were countless times when family members would buy her school supplies, clothes, and even food. It was through the compassion of her family that she saw the love of Jesus on full display.

It's easy to see a family member in physical need and respond with a platitude like, "I will pray for God to provide." But have you ever thought that his provision might come through you? Praying for someone is far more comfortable than giving away your own resources. Yet Jesus calls us to act on our compassion. As John explains, we should not merely love with words and speech but with action in truth.

## Prayer

*Father, would you open my eyes and heart to see the needs of my family? I don't want my compassion toward my family to be limited to their spiritual needs. I want to be a generous person who willingly shares the resources you have given me. Guide me to opportunities to show compassion toward my family. Amen.*

## Prompt

Spend some time thinking about the needs of your family members. Who comes to mind? As you think about your family's current situation and their needs, can you see any ways you can help them? Over the next week, ask God to show you how you can care for someone in your family with no strings attached.

# Compassion for the One Who Won't Listen

*Know this, my beloved brothers: let every person be quick to hear, slow to speak, slow to anger.*

James 1:19, English Standard Version

These words of James are often quoted, yet they can be the hardest ones to implement. It's difficult to be quick to listen and slow to speak when all you're trying to do is get someone to understand where you are coming from.

It's hard when you're trying to explain to your kid why they can't do something they really want to do. Or when you're trying to have a conversation with a family member who has different religious beliefs. Or when you're having a moral disagreement with a sibling. Or when that one family member brings up politics again and is relentless in sharing their point of view but won't listen to anyone else.

Family is complicated. You don't get to select who's in your family, and the range of beliefs, moral standards, and life philosophies can stretch far and wide.

But in these situations, when all you want is be heard, Jesus is calling you to be quicker to listen and slower to speak. It's not because what you have to say doesn't matter. It's because you're more likely to gain a listening ear if you first show that you want to hear what they have to say.

It doesn't matter if you completely disagree with them. Just listen. Allow them to express their side openly, without trying to get your next word in. You will find listening to someone will help you earn trust and sometimes a listening ear in return. You are not alone in your desire to be heard. You just have to choose to be the one to listen.

## Prayer

*Lord, would you help me be slow to speak and quick to listen? I want to be someone to whom my family can turn and know that I will hear them. Even with the most difficult person in my family—with whom I often disagree on everything—I want to hear them, too. Would you remind me to listen before I speak? Amen.*

## Prompt

What would it look like if you tried to listen more today? To whom can you actively choose to listen instead of speak? Step into your next conversation with a family member and actively choose to listen to them. When you're mindful of listening, you might realize that you're not as good at it as you thought.

# Making Sacrifices for Your Family's Health

*Do nothing out of selfish ambition or vain conceit.*
*Rather, in humility value others above yourselves, not*
*looking to your own interests but each of you to the*
*interests of the others.*

*Philippians 2:3–4, New International Version*

One of Tamara's biggest challenges while newly married was adjusting to being mindful of another person. She was used to making last-minute decisions to visit friends or going wherever she wanted after work. It's not that she couldn't do those things anymore, but she needed to be mindful of Dale and their time together.

When it comes to family, you sometimes have to give up what you would prefer for the greater good of everyone else. Being compassionate to your family means thinking of them first.

In his letter to the church in Philippi, Paul says that humility is the key to succeeding in this principle. If you genuinely think of others more highly than yourself, it's easy to prioritize the needs of your family over your own momentary preferences.

Choosing to always think of your family's overall health before your own desires is a pretty countercultural idea in our very individualistic society. But sacrificing and putting others first will actually make your family stronger and unite you in ways you didn't know were possible.

Of course, it's important for every member of the family to care for all the others. But it starts with you. As you're on

20   PRACTICING CHRISTIAN COMPASSION

this journey toward being the compassionate person you are called to be, you'll have to be the initiator. It really is remarkable to see how your sacrifices become contagious as other members of your family choose to embark upon their own journeys toward compassion.

It doesn't matter what your role is in your family; you can make sacrifices for the overall health of everyone. This might mean cancelling your plans so that you can be present with someone who has had a hard day. It might mean pausing your favorite show just to listen. Sacrifice isn't easy, but it's what you're called to do for others—and that includes your family.

## Prayer

*God, I want to be a person who extends compassion to my family. Would you reveal to me the areas in my life I need to sacrifice for them? Would you show me if there are any areas that I'm being selfish and, in turn, compromising my family's overall health? Amen.*

## Prompt

Make a list of your family's current needs. They could be physical, mental, emotional, or financial. It could be a need of one person in your family. Once you've made the list, see if there's one or two things on it that you could help with. If it means giving up something of your own, pray about letting it go for the good of your family.

# Navigating a Family Death with Care

*Rejoice with those who rejoice; mourn with those who mourn.*

*Romans 12:15, New International Version*

Dealing with loss is never easy. When you lose someone, it's natural to forget the struggle that others in your family are going through. As you try to process loss for yourself, you might find it difficult to be compassionate and empathetic toward others who are grieving in your family. We all mourn in our own ways, but we need to learn to mourn *with* one another. One of the greatest forms of compassion comes through empathy in moments of crisis.

Tamara lost her mom at a young age. That season of life was an absolutely devastating time for her, and she quickly realized that no two people grieve the same way. For at least a year, she was very angry and took it out on everyone around her, especially other members in her family. It wasn't until years later that she realized she wasn't the only one who lost someone important. Other members of her family were grieving, and she never showed compassion for them and their process.

It's important to allow yourself to grieve the loss of a family member. But in that process, it's equally important to remember that others are grieving a loss, as well.

Instead of isolating yourself and assuming you have no one to go to, you can mourn alongside other family members. If you're having a hard day, it's likely they are, too.

22   PRACTICING CHRISTIAN COMPASSION

If you are remembering a special event or memory, it's likely they are, too. A small measure of compassion for another family member during this time will go a long way toward their healing process, as well as your own.

## Prayer

*God, you are the God of all comfort, and I need your comfort in this hour. Continue to draw me closer to you and allow me to find your peace that surpasses understanding. Even as I'm filled with great heartache, I know I'm not the only one. Would you be the tower of refuge for my family members? It's only through your comfort and strength that I will be able to show compassion toward others as I grieve the loss of someone I love. Amen.*

## Prompt

There's no right way to grieve, but there are helpful ways to process your emotions. Dedicate two days out of this week to write down everything you are feeling, good or bad. Write until you've gotten everything out. After you finish writing, take a moment to think of one other family member who is grieving during this time. How can you reach out to them this week? Would you call them, write them a note, or maybe even send them a meal? Choose one act of compassion that you can carry out for them this week.

# Being Present for the Drama of Family Gatherings

*And above all these put on love, which binds everything together in perfect harmony.*

Colossians 3:14, English Standard Version

Compassion seeks to bring us closer together at times when it would be easier to withdraw. We all naturally lean away from pain, and it can be especially tempting to disengage when your entire family is gathered together with all its dysfunction on full display.

At least, that's the way Dale feels. He grew up in a family rife with interpersonal turmoil. Abuse, alcoholism, divorce, and narcissism were all part of his childhood family culture. To protect himself, he sometimes found it easier to disengage from relationships with emotionally unhealthy family members. In some cases, he found it easy to let them continue saying harmful or untrue things without attempting to understand their point of view or share his own. With other relationships, he learned to avoid certain family members entirely.

We're often tempted to disengage because it can be difficult to see a future where things in your family will be any better—any *healthier*. It's so easy to get cynical.

But cynicism is the enemy of compassion. Whereas cynicism is marked by the walls you put up around your heart to keep from getting hurt, compassion cultivates the vulnerability that is necessary to step deeper into the hurts, pains, and messiness of the lives of others. Compassion produces a willingness to get hurt if, in the process, there's a possibility of helping someone else grow in love. As Paul encourages us in Colossians, love binds all things together in harmony.

There is no better place to practice this kind of love than at the next family gathering, where old drama crops up anew and tempers flare in predictable ways. In those moments when you feel weary from your family's brokenness, actively choose to clothe yourself with love. It has the power to bind all things together, and that includes you and your family.

## Prayer

*Father God, give me the strength to lean in when things get uncomfortable. Empower me to absorb pain and maintain healthy vulnerability. Guard my heart from cynicism, and as I lean into my family's brokenness, may they experience the healing that only you can bring. Amen.*

## Prompt

Pray about how you can reconnect with a family member from whom you've recently been distant. Find a way to extend an olive branch. As you do, prepare yourself for the possibility that they won't respond the way you had hoped, but resolve to remain vulnerable anyway.

## THE BENEFITS
## OF COMPASSION

It's clear that Jesus has called us to compassion and self-sacrifice for the good of others. In fact, his entire life was marked by it. He healed the sick. He identified with the marginalized. He sat and wept with those who were hurting. Ultimately, he gave his life so that anyone who puts their trust in him might experience an end to their pain and brokenness.

To be sure, compassion is difficult. It's such a weighty calling. But God doesn't call us into difficult lifestyle choices without good reason. His commands aren't arbitrary. Jesus is always inviting you to do the right thing, and, as it turns out, the right thing can be challenging, but also is good for you.

When you choose compassion, you choose to stand with someone. You identify with them and form a deeper connection with them. In a world plagued by isolation and loneliness, perhaps the answer to what ails us is less about seeking personal fulfillment and more about being willing to stand together in our burdens.

When we lean into deeper connection with others, pain will always be present because we're broken and sinful people, living in a fallen world. But if we're willing to experience the pain, we will also experience a richness of life that we would not have known otherwise.

That's why, in Matthew 10:39 (New International Version), Jesus said:

*"Whoever finds their life will lose it, and whoever loses their life for my sake will find it."*

## CHAPTER TWO

# FRIENDS

**Of all the relational** connections we have, friendship plays an especially important role. It has often been said that while you're born into your family of origin, friends are the family you get to choose. In light of this, it's vital that we nurture these relationships with compassion.

People long to be connected to others and experience an abiding sense of belonging, and that's actually by design. God has wired us for community. It's an integral part of our life and self-identity.

It's no secret that cultivating deep and lasting relationships requires intention, and that's especially true of your friendships. While you might feel a certain urgency to rectify relational rifts with your family members, that same sense of urgency isn't always present in friendships. It's often far easier to let a friendship die than to enter into the hard work of talking through differences and disagreements. We encourage you to challenge yourself to show compassion and understanding during instances such as these.

If you're willing to cultivate unwavering compassion for your friends, you'll find that difficult and uncomfortable seasons will strengthen your bond. We all want to feel connection, but connection is preceded by compassion and empathy.

It won't always feel like it in the moment, but the benefits of compassionate friendship are well worth the effort they require. True friendship is a place of safety, honesty, and love. Your friends are the people who will show up for you at two in the morning or when you find yourself in the midst of a crisis and need someone to talk to. Friends are the people you can share your struggles with and seek advice from when you feel like you don't have anyone to turn to.

Family is a foundational part of life, but we should never neglect our friends. Even Jesus valued his friendships. He selected twelve men with whom he spent a majority of his time, and three within those twelve were his closest friends: James, John, and Peter. They were the ones who caught a glimpse of his glory at his transfiguration, and they were the ones he asked to sit and pray with him on the darkest night of his life. When it comes to caring for friends, Jesus shows us that you need to be there in both the highest and lowest moments.

You can unknowingly harm your friendships by not being present in the ways your friends need most. To build lasting friendships, you must be mindful of challenges and work through them. Let's explore what that looks like.

# Compassion When You're Not Invited

*Be completely humble and gentle; be patient, bearing with one another in love.*

Ephesians 4:2, New International Version

Last year, a friend of Dale's announced their wedding engagement, and he was thrilled. Dale assumed that he would be asked to be part of the celebration, perhaps even to officiate. But he wasn't, and that hurt.

Nobody likes to be left out, and in key moments of life, thoughtless gestures—or lack of gestures—can ruin a relationship. It can be painful to be excluded from the wedding party of someone you thought you were close to, like Dale experienced. Maybe you weren't even invited to the wedding. Or perhaps a friend bought the products or services of someone else in your line of work instead of coming to you.

In times like these, you might feel betrayed because you thought you and your friend were closer than they apparently did. Other times, you might feel embarrassed because you thought that you were more important or influential in someone's life than you actually were.

It can be hard to know what led to this mismatch of expectations. But in order to move past hurt feelings and toward relational healing, you'll need to work to see the situation from their perspective. Maybe they were overstressed. If it was their wedding, maybe they were over budget. Perhaps they made an honest mistake in overlooking you. Or, as hard as it is to admit, maybe you just haven't been there for them as much as you thought, and that's why they didn't include you.

Whatever the case, you need to be able to see the world from their eyes and let go of your own ego and need to be right. Paul encourages us to bear with one another, and that means assuming the best of others' intentions rather than viewing the situation through the lens of our own hurt.

Humility, gentleness, and patience go a long way in helping us do that. When you see the world from the perspective of your friend, even though they hurt you, you're better equipped to bear with them in love.

## Prayer

*God, allow me to see past my hurt in order to understand my friend's perspective. Show me ways that I can promote healing and understanding rather than blaming or distancing. Help me own my shortcomings and bear with my friend in love. Amen.*

## Prompt

If you've recently been hurt by a friend who didn't invite you or reach out to you when you thought they would, ask yourself why that might be. What can you do to get the relationship to where you thought it already was or accept what it currently is? What can you own? Pray about reaching out to that friend to debrief the situation with them in a nonjudgmental way to see and understand their perspective.

# Empathy for the Friend
# in a Different Life Stage

*There is a time for everything, and a season for every*
*activity under the heavens.*

Ecclesiastes 3:1, New International Version

The ancient wisdom of Solomon teaches us that life is never
stagnant. The world is always in motion, and every season
of life is just that: a season. This is a major theme throughout
the book of Ecclesiastes. Solomon often repeats that life is a
vapor; it has an ephemeral quality to it. You can see, observe,
and interact with it, but you can't ever grasp it or keep it from
shifting and moving.

If you fail to remember this truth when it comes to your
friendships, you might find your feelings are often hurt.
You're hurt when your relationships change, because you
see your friendships as a place of safety and comfort, while
change is scary and uncomfortable. But you need to always
allow for the possibility (actually, the sure reality) that friendships change and evolve as much as the people in them.

In times of transition, it's important to focus on how you
can be there for your friend rather than all the ways you
want them to be there for you. That isn't always easy.
You might feel a sense of loss when your friend finds a significant other or gets married and now has less time to spend
with you. Double that when they start having kids. Or maybe
you're the one with a spouse and a baby, and you feel like
your single friend just doesn't understand.

As you come to grips with the changing landscape of your
close friendships, it's okay to mourn the end of a season that

you sincerely enjoyed. But don't stay there. Learn to love your friend in this new phase of life. Seek to build your friendship in brand new ways. Even though both you and your friend might feel some relational growing pains, if you show them how much you love them during this time, they will never forget it.

## Prayer

*God, give me empathy for my friends in seasons of life transition. Keep my feelings of loss from turning into resentment. Help me lean into my relationships rather than leaning away from the pain. Teach me how to be the kind of friend I need to be in this season. Amen.*

## Prompt

Think about a friend that you're feeling distant from because of a recent life transition. Commit to praying for them and let them know that you're doing so. Pay attention to the pain and stress in their life and commit to be there for them in those places, even if you're feeling hurt right now.

# Being the Family
# Your Friend Doesn't Have

*One who has unreliable friends soon comes to ruin, but*
*there is a friend who sticks closer than a brother.*

*Proverbs 18:24, New International Version*

Dale doesn't have very much family support. He's always
relied on his friends to share the big moments of his life.
Whether it's enduring difficult times, celebrating a victory
such as college graduation, or something that's a little of
both such as having a newborn baby, Dale has shared those
moments in far more meaningful ways with his friends
than with his family of origin.

Success often isn't determined as much by what you do
as it is by who you surround yourself with. Perhaps that's
why this proverbial wisdom from Solomon rings so true. If
you have unreliable friends, you may find yourself in a difficult situation without any support. But there are friends who
can end up being closer to you than your own sibling. We
don't know anyone who doesn't want that.

But in order to *have* a friend, you need to first *be* a friend.
You can't expect people to be meaningfully invested in
your life if you don't meaningfully invest in theirs. Seek to
be the kind of friend you want to have. Be the one who's
the first to show up to help, even when your friend didn't
ask for it. Always be willing to lend a helping hand, even
when it's inconvenient for you. Whether it's bringing a meal,
offering to babysit, or calling to pray and encourage, seek
to go above and beyond what's expected of you. This drives
deeper relationships.

When you do these things, don't keep score. Express love through your actions. If you do that, you'll never be lacking for friends who are closer than family.

*God, make me the kind of friend I need others to be for me. Help me do it unselfishly and purely for the good of the other person. Teach me how to truly love my friends in both the highs and lows of life. Give me insight to know how to practically do just that. Amen.*

Choose one thing you can do this week for a friend that you previously might have only thought to do for a family member. If you're not sure what that looks like, try to think back on a time when you felt really loved by a close friend. Let that memory inspire you with ideas for what you might do to be a friend who sticks closer than a sibling.

# Loving Your Friends' Kids as if They Were Your Own

*This man had a very beautiful and lovely young cousin, Hadassah, who was also called Esther. When her father and mother died, Mordecai adopted her into his family and raised her as his own daughter.*

Esther 2:7, New Living Translation

When a man named Mordecai found out that his uncle and aunt had passed away and left his little cousin, Esther, without any parents, it must have been a shock. But immediately after their deaths, Mordecai took Esther in and cared for her as though she were his own daughter. He became an incredibly influential figure in her life. And when God called Esther to do something great for her people, she wouldn't have been able to do it if Mordecai had not been there to guide her.

In the same way Mordecai cared for Esther and had an influence in her life, you, too, can care for the children of your friends. Your role in the life of your friend isn't limited to the relationship with your friend; it extends to their family and children. Just about every parent would agree that one of the best ways to love them is to first love their children.

We're all called to raise up the next generation in the ways of Jesus. If we think that duty rests solely on the shoulders of parents for the benefit of only their own children, we're thinking far too narrowly.

You might never fully understand the impact you can make by modeling the love of Jesus to your friends' children. Parents need other adults to stand alongside them and to love and guide their children. One of the greatest ways you can support your friend is by being there for their children.

## Prayer

*Father, give me a heart for the children who are not my own. Allow my love for you to pour out into the lives of my friends' children. I want them to see my love for their parents and my love for you by the way I interact with them. Give me a heart of sincerity and genuine love for my friends' children. Amen.*

## Prompt

Think of one of your friends who has children. Do you know their kids well? Or have you failed to interact with them on a deep level? Find one step you can take to develop a relationship with your friend's children. It might look like engaging in conversation with them when you visit your friend or maybe taking them out for a small activity they would enjoy. Find one thing you can do and plan to make it happen this month.

# Navigating a Friend's Divorce

*He heals the brokenhearted and binds up their wounds.*

*Psalm 147:3, New International Version*

Life is messy, and recovering from certain wounds is harder than others. Psalm 147 beautifully expresses something that we often have a hard time believing: God is near. He's not somewhere in the clouds, far away from his people. On the contrary, he cares deeply for you. He sees your heartache. And not only does he see it, he feels it alongside you. This is the kind of love God has given us to express in our friendships, especially in the darkest moments of life.

Regardless of your stance on divorce, it's clear that it brings so much pain and suffering. Having served as a pastor, Dale has attended or taken part in the wedding of couples only to see them divorce a few years later. Divorce is a tragedy, and it hurts so bad to watch it unfold up close. If you have a friend going through a divorce, your advice and opinions are probably less helpful than you might think.

What your friend needs is a nonjudgmental, listening presence. Not someone who takes sides, but someone who listens well. Even if you don't agree with how your friend has acted in the midst of their divorce conflict, you can still offer comfort. You can share compassion during a time when they need it the most.

The road to your friend's healing and restoration will be long, but you can join them on that journey. Allow God to use you in the process. It might be through your friendship that God begins to heal their broken heart and bind up their wounds. This situation is larger than you are, but that doesn't mean God can't use you.

Displaying the tender heart of Jesus during a difficult time in your friend's life speaks louder than your opposition or opinion of the situation. To support your friend's healing doesn't mean you're supporting every decision they've made. Model Jesus in their hour of need.

## Prayer

*Father, you know what my friend is enduring far better than I ever could. I ask that you give me a heart of compassion toward them and that you give me words of wisdom when we talk. Would you use me in this hour to shine your light of love and comfort? It's only through you that I can put my personal opinions aside and be what my friend needs. Amen.*

## Prompt

Do you have a friend in your life going through a divorce? If not, maybe think of a friend who is enduring a relational strain. What's one act of compassion you can extend to your friend?

## SELF-COMPASSION TIP

As you cultivate compassion, it's important to remember that you won't always get it right. There are times when you will say or do something hurtful, thoughtless, or unempathetic. In these moments, remind yourself that the message of Jesus is one of forgiveness.

And though we may stand firm in our belief in forgiving others, we often have difficulty showing ourselves the same kindness. It's easy to get discouraged and disheartened by our own failures and shortcomings. Set out each day with the intention of being as forgiving to yourself as you are toward others in your life.

# Learning to Love the Differences Between You And Your Friends

*For Christ himself has brought peace to us. He united Jews and Gentiles into one people when, in his own body on the cross, he broke down the wall of hostility that separated us.*

*Ephesians 2:14, New Living Translation*

It's only natural to cultivate deep relationships with people with whom you feel comfortable. Perhaps you gravitate toward those who have similar life experiences, family dynamics, or who generally share the same politics and life philosophies.

There's nothing inherently wrong with building friend-ships with people we can easily relate to, but if you're a follower of Jesus, you've been given a *supernatural* ability to do something even better. It's written into the DNA of what it means to be a Christian.

When Jesus began his ministry, he spoke to a mostly Jewish audience. But he always had an international vision for the Church. Remember, at that time Jewish people didn't associate with non-Jews, or vice versa. In fact, they were openly hostile toward one another.

But by his death and resurrection, Jesus has broken down that dividing wall of hostility. He made it possible for you to enter into deep relationships with people who look nothing like you—people from different cultures, political parties, and family upbringings. God brings people together through their common bond in Jesus.

Dale and Tamara have experienced this firsthand. Some of our closest friends come from different cultures, ethnicities, socioeconomic statuses, generations, and upbringings. In cultivating deep relationships across these differences, we've learned and grown so much. We honestly thank God for our differences.

Jesus is inviting you to experience unity where there was once hostility and aversion. If you're willing to befriend people who are nothing like you, you will begin to see a fuller picture of the humanity that is created in the image of God.

## Prayer

*Heavenly Father, I ask that you grant me opportunities to develop feelings of tolerance, patience, and compassion for those who think differently from me. And may that be a testament to how your love transforms not only my life as an individual, but how you can transform the Church as a community. Let me see that power firsthand. Amen.*

## Prompt

Take a look at the people you hang out with most. Do they all look, talk, and think like you? If so, pray about someone in your life who's different from you—someone from whom you want to learn and with whom you want to cultivate a friendship. Then, reach out to them to see if they want to get together for coffee or lunch. Ask them about their life and begin trying to see the world through their eyes.

# Sacrificing for Your Friends

*Greater love has no one than this: to lay down one's life for one's friends.*

John 15:13, New International Version

Love and sacrifice always go hand-in-hand. This is what Jesus modeled for us perfectly when he laid down his own life so that we might experience eternal life. And he's calling us into a lifestyle that's willing to make the same kind of sacrifice for others.

Now, loving your friend might not ever mean literally laying down your physical life, but it will require very real sacrifice. As you seek to be with your friend in moments of need, you might have to give up something you cherish. In order to truly support your friend, you might need to give up your time, rest, finances, and comfort.

Tamara has a friend who has modeled great sacrifice on her behalf for the sake of their friendship. There are count-less moments she could share, but one stood out to her the most. Tamara was in labor with her first child and delivered her baby at two in the morning. Her friend had waited up all night to hear when the baby arrived, and as soon as she heard the baby was born, she jumped out of her pajamas, drove 30 miles, navigated a dark hospital, and congratulated Tamara on her new baby. She didn't stay too long because she wanted to give Tamara a chance to rest. She went back home, slept for a few short hours, and then went to work. She sacrificed a lot to be there for Tamara on a day when she needed her.

Sacrificing for friends isn't fun or easy, but there are moments when you'll need to do something that shows how much you love them. To extend compassion is to make sacrifices that have no benefit for you. Let your love come with no strings attached and no expectations. This is what Jesus wants our friendships to look like.

## Prayer

*God, thank you for sending your Son to model the greatest form of sacrifice we will ever know. I'm grateful that you've made me aware of my need to follow after Jesus and sacrifice for my friends. I ask that you would reveal my own heart to me and show me where I've been selfish in my friendships. Show me where I need to make sacrifices so that my friends will know I'm here for them and that I love them. Amen.*

## Prompt

Write down the last time one of your friends made a sacrifice for you. Then, write down the last time you made a sacrifice for one of your friends. If it was harder for you to think of a moment you sacrificed for your friend, then bring that before God. Take a moment to ask him to show you how you can make genuine sacrifices for your friend.

# Forgiving Your Friends' Faults

*Make allowance for each other's faults, and forgive anyone who offends you. Remember, the Lord forgave you, so you must forgive others.*

Colossians 3:13, New Living Translation

When you come to faith in Jesus, everything about your life profoundly changes. You begin to behave in a way that seems almost bizarre to those who don't follow Jesus. One key transformation in your life is how you respond when someone offends you. When you think about the measure of forgiveness that Jesus gave you, it's an extraordinary kind of forgiveness. In his letter to the Colossians, Paul calls us to be equally extraordinary in the forgiveness we give to others.

In any friendship, hurt feelings are inevitable, but our response should always be to forgive with the same measure of forgiveness that Jesus has given us. That's not easy. Forgiveness means dealing with a wound rather than covering it up. In the short term, the process of forgiveness can be far more painful than simply holding a grudge. But in the end, it brings freedom and healing. Holding a grudge will never offer you those things.

Jesus is calling us to extend forgiveness not because the other person deserves it, but because he forgave you for far greater things. The wellspring of forgiveness that he has extended to you is the source from which your forgiveness for others must flow.

Sometimes, you don't want to engage in the process of forgiveness because you aren't sure how refusing to ignore a hurt might change your friendship. Tamara knows what that's like. One time, her friend took some actions that made her feel like the friendship was slowly ending, and instead of bringing it up, she settled in her heart that this was just how it was going to be.

But then, an opportunity came for her to share how she felt with her friend. In that moment, it became clear that it was all a big misunderstanding and completely unintentional. Through that conversation, their friendship was restored and forgiveness was extended.

It isn't always a large offense for which you are harboring unforgiveness. Sometimes, it's small and seems relatively harmless. Being a good friend means expecting that disagreements will come and being determined to work through them. One of the greatest forms of compassion you can show your friend is being willing to extend forgiveness when you're offended rather than harboring bitterness.

## Prayer

*Lord, help me extend forgiveness to my friends. When the temptation to hold a grudge lurks in my heart, remind me that you have forgiven me of far greater things. Make me more like you. May forgiveness be my first response. Amen.*

## Prompt

Take a moment to search your heart and see if you are holding any grudges against a friend. Contact them in order to reconcile the unforgiveness in your heart.

# Sitting in Your Friends' Suffering

*Then they sat on the ground with him for seven days and seven nights. No one said a word to him, because they saw how great his suffering was.*

Job 2:13, New International Version

Perhaps the most famous story of suffering in the Bible is that of Job. Job was a man of wealth and influence who had lived his life as uprightly as he could. He loved God, and he loved his family. And yet, one day, he found himself suffering more than he could bear. His children died in an accident, his wealth suddenly vanished, and even his physical health began to fail.

During this time, three of Job's friends visited him. What they did when they arrived might seem strange, but it was the best thing they could have possibly done. They sat with him in silence for an entire week. They didn't say a single thing to him for seven days. They just sat with him in sorrow.

This was their shining moment, because when they eventually did start talking to Job, they led him to an even darker place than he had been before.

Too often, we think that we need to fix our friends' problems—give them advice, help them with a plan of attack, come save the day—but maybe they don't need that from you. Maybe they just need you to sit with them in silence. In his years serving as a pastor, Dale has come to understand the value of silent support in times of great pain.

So, be a silent supporter. Sit quietly with your friend in the hospital room, by the graveside, or in the midst of a breakup or emotional turmoil. Don't try to conjure up something poetic or even biblical to say. Just be there with them. It's likely what they need more than anything else you have to offer. Oftentimes, people don't feel the warmth of God's presence until they feel the warmth of a friend who is simply willing to be there.

## Prayer

*Father God, help me step into the painful experiences of my friends. Teach me when to keep my mouth shut. Allow me to bring a sense of peace to every difficult situation. May my presence speak louder than my words ever could. Amen.*

## Prompt

The next time you're consoling a friend, be intentional about allowing space for silence. Don't let it make you uncomfortable. Don't try to think of something to say or fill the silence. Have the discipline to be present in the moment with your friend, whatever they may be feeling.

# Compassion When Your Friend Makes a Bad Life Choice

In a world of cancel culture, Twitter wars, and partisan hostility, the voice of the Christian must always be filled with grace, particularly when we're talking to people who don't share all of our beliefs.

Whether your friends are believers or not, they won't always share your outlook on life. They'll make decisions or choices that you simply don't agree with. You might even be able to see the negative impact of their choices long before they do, so you may wonder what role you could play in bringing that to their attention.

Tamara has often struggled when people close to her make poor life decisions that lead to predictably painful outcomes. It could be an unwise romantic entanglement, a financially foolish choice, or a bad career move. In those moments, she intentionally has to remind herself to be there for her friends rather than sharing her unheard wisdom.

Of course, you love and care for your friend and want the best for them, but that doesn't always mean your words will come across that way. It's important to be sure that your words are full of grace. In your friendships, you should be able to speak truth and wisdom without fear. That said, you should also be mindful of *how* you're speaking. If your friend is making a terrible life choice, you might feel tempted to correct them. That opportunity may present itself, but you have to be mindful of how you offer correction or guidance.

Friendships are built on trust. We're called to speak wisdom to the people closest to us, but it's important to avoid damaging a relationship because you "spoke truth" in an uncompassionate way. In his letter to the Colossians, Paul says our words should be seasoned with salt, meaning they should have a preserving nature to them. Be compassionate in your offering of correction and wisdom. Let your words show grace and love rather than judgment.

## Prayer

*God, I see the decision my friend is making, and it pains me. As I desire to share wisdom, would you guide me? I want my words to come across with grace and love. I want my friend to know that I am on their side and truly caring for their good. Would you make me sensitive and mindful to the delicacy of this situation? Amen.*

## Prompt

Do you have a friend who has been making some bad life choices? Think about the truth you want to share with them and the manner in which you want to share it. Understanding what might trigger your friend, think about what words you should avoid. Write down your heart's true intention for correcting your friend. If it's simply for the sake of telling them they're wrong, then it's probably best you say nothing at all.

# THE BENEFITS
# OF COMPASSION

In life, most of us want to feel happy and secure, and we know that finding this kind of fulfillment takes more than simply having a good job and a nice place to live. It even requires more than having a great marriage and good kids. We also need to experience connectedness with the world outside our homes.

Although it may seem counterintuitive, the best way to feel fulfilled is simply to seek to see the world from the perspective of others and to serve them in those spaces. This drives deeper connection, which brings both a sense of fulfillment and security.

Unless you have deep and lasting friendships built on compassion, you'll always feel like something's missing. This is the wisdom of the ancients, as explained in Ecclesiastes 4:9–10 (New International Version):

*"Two are better than one, because they have a good return for their labor: If either of them falls down, one can help the other up. But pity anyone who falls and has no one to help them up."*

If you build compassionate friendships, you will be able to accomplish more than you could on your own, and you'll have someone to share the journey with. Success in life isn't determined by what you can get but by what you can give. When you have a posture of giving, you'll always have more than enough.

## CHAPTER THREE

# COLLEAGUES AND COWORKERS

**As you begin looking** to spread compassion outside of your close circle of family and friends, you may immediately be tempted to think about the wider community or even global compassion efforts. And those are certainly important areas that we'll get to later in this book.

Before we get there, however, we want to spend some time thinking intentionally about how you can make an impact in the place where you probably spend most of your waking hours: at work. It's all too easy to overlook the incredible opportunities you have to show the heart of Jesus to those you see every day in your office or workplace. In order to become a truly compassionate person, you need to focus your energy on being not only a good employee but also a compassionate one.

More often than not, we focus on all the ways our coworkers get under our skin. You may complain about their daily habits or idiosyncrasies. Or maybe you bemoan the fact that your organization's office space is small and you feel cramped in the workspace you have to share with a colleague. Perhaps you don't think your boss is a competent leader. Or maybe you feel like you deserved a promotion that went to somebody else. These are all often subjects of complaint when you get home and talk to your spouse, sibling, or roommate. The fact of the matter is, you'll always find ways to be annoyed with people you spend all day with.

But what if you looked at the circumstances in your workplace differently? What if, instead of seeing all these relational dynamics as points of contention, you see them as opportunities for compassion? Being in close proximity to the same people every day gives you an incredible opportunity to create relational depth with them that can serve as the breeding ground for life-changing compassion. In order to do that, you'll need to worry less about what you can and can't get out of your coworkers and more about what you're able to offer them.

Whether or not you find your work fulfilling, you have the opportunity to improve the lives of those who work alongside you. To a certain extent, you're stuck with them, but that doesn't have to be a bad thing. You have a captive audience. Rather than plaguing them with negativity, breathe life into them with compassion. Maybe it's time to begin thinking of yourself as having two full-time jobs: the role you currently serve in, and your self-appointed new role as Chief Compassion Officer.

As we begin this chapter, we invite you to stop seeing your colleagues simply as fellow workers performing functions in an organization and to start seeing them as people created in the image of God. Remember that your coworkers are human beings with many of the same hopes, dreams, worries, and fears that you have. They need compassion, and, for 40 hours a week, you can help give it to them.

# Caring Enough to Know
# Your Coworkers

*Live in harmony with one another. Do not be haughty,*
*but associate with the lowly. Never be wise in your*
*own sight.*

Romans 12:16, English Standard Version

Living as a Christian in everyday settings means living in harmony with the people around you—*all* the people around you. That's Paul's encouragement to the church in Rome: to be intentional about creating a shared bond based on trust and humility. As a follower of Jesus, the way you live alongside others should look like caring for them rather than simply existing next to them.

When it comes to people you work with on a daily basis, it's easy to show up and leave without ever really knowing anyone. Yet Jesus wants us to live in true harmony with one another and interact with people we naturally wouldn't. No matter what your position in your workplace or organization looks like, it's important to take a moment to get to know the people you see every day.

You don't really get to choose your coworkers, and maybe that's a good thing. It presents an opportunity to associate with people you normally wouldn't come across. Having a diverse workplace encourages you to establish relationships with people who don't necessarily think, talk, believe, or act like you. And it doesn't have to be hard. Dale often uses the few minutes just before a meeting to chat and ask coworkers questions about themselves and their lives.

The call to care for others isn't restricted to certain social groups. It extends to every part of our lives. Oftentimes, we don't think to move past work-related conversations and step into a deeper form of connection with our coworkers; if we did, we might be pleasantly surprised by the relationships we'd begin to build with them. More of our time is spent at work than any other single location, and that alone provides opportunities to connect with people on a deeper level.

## Prayer

*Lord, thank you for placing me in a workplace where I have the opportunity to get to know other people. I ask that you would give me a heart to know more about those I work with every day. Would you provide opportunities for me to engage deeper with my colleagues and show me ways to extend genuine care toward them? Amen.*

## Prompt

Think of one person at work, school, or in another setting whom you frequently see but don't know well. Who is that person and what do you know about them? How can you engage in intentional conversation with them?

# When You Don't Get Along with Your Colleague

*But love your enemies, do good to them, and lend to them without expecting to get anything back. Then your reward will be great, and you will be children of the Most High, because he is kind to the ungrateful and wicked.*

Luke 6:35, New International Version

Life can be difficult when you don't get along with your coworkers, so it's in your best interest to make friends with them, and not just because life will be better for you. You will also be able to bring about good in your coworkers' lives by being an ally to them.

It's tempting to find ways to complain about coworkers you don't like and to even find ways to undercut them. Tamara felt that temptation while working at a Christian camp with one employee she found to be particularly lazy. She couldn't stand him!

But Jesus's words show us a new way to overcome this temptation. Instead of seeking to undercut or even just flat out avoiding coworkers whom you don't naturally like, actively seek their good.

The reason that Jesus gives for this command is just as poignant. God himself is kind to the ungrateful and the wicked. While you may feel inclined to call your coworkers ungrateful and wicked—and whether that's a fair assessment or not—he still calls you to show them kindness. After all, hasn't he shown you kindness when you did not deserve it?

Once Tamara got to know the coworker she didn't like on a personal level, they actually became friends. And when she moved on to another job, he was one of the people she was sad to leave.

Jesus is calling you to move toward the coworkers you simply cannot stand. If you're faithful to respond to that call, you'll be glad you did, and your reward will be great.

## Prayer

*Father God, make me more gracious and compassionate to the coworker with whom I don't get along. Help me see their actions through a more charitable lens. And even when I feel like I have been wronged, help me give only goodness in return. Amen.*

## Prompt

Think about a coworker whom you cannot stand. Think about all the ways they annoy you. Then, begin praying that God would bless them, and the next time you see them at work, find a tangible way to bless them yourself. Go out of your way to show them kindness. Look for opportunities to do something good for them without expecting anything in return.

# Be the Workplace Encourager

*Dear brothers and sisters, I close my letter with these last words: Be joyful. Grow to maturity. Encourage each other. Live in harmony and peace. Then the God of love and peace will be with you.*

2 Corinthians 13:11, New Living Translation

Everyone needs encouragement, but it isn't always easy to come by, especially in the workplace. Paul's final words to the church of Corinth come with a call for believers to be people of joy, maturity, and encouragement. These virtues don't necessarily come naturally to us, but they are markers of the new person Jesus is creating us to be.

Negative attitudes are contagious. It's usually way easier to be negative than encouraging. Dale enjoys spreading negativity more than he'd like to admit. He's pretty good natured and makes a lot of jokes because he's a class clown of sorts. But too often, he weaponizes his humor to highlight the ways he's dissatisfied with whatever's happening in the workplace.

This tendency toward negativity is a representation of our unredeemed selves, the parts of our humanity of which we must let go. Jesus is inviting us to live a life full of abundance and joy as we engage in relationships with other people. A key component of that life is having a spirit of encouragement. This doesn't mean you have to lack authenticity and genuineness for the sake of always being nice. Instead, Paul is really urging us to find moments and opportunities to be genuinely encouraging.

When stress is piled high and tension is thick, find a way to be a voice of genuine encouragement to your colleagues.

Difficult situations are bound to present themselves, but you have a choice about how you will respond. Not only will you see the personal benefits of seeking out moments of encouragement, but the people around you will benefit, as well. You have no idea how God will use your words of encouragement to meet someone where they are and show them his love.

## Prompt

Today, a moment of frustration will come. In that moment, choose to pause. Truly think about your view on the situation. In what way can you choose to speak words of encouragement? Once you've thought about what to say, actually say it to your colleague.

# Cultivate a Culture of "We're All in This Together"

*And let us consider how we may spur one another on toward love and good deeds.*

Hebrews 10:24, New International Version

Working toward a common goal has a way of unifying you and the other members of your team. That's exactly what the author of Hebrews is highlighting: working together to see something good.

During her time in college, Tamara's least favorite assignments were group projects. She didn't want her grade to depend on the work and effort of other students. She wanted full control over the outcome. But that's not how the real world works. In the real world, we have to work with other people. From sports to companies to throwing an event, we have to rely on others to accomplish the same goal.

Learning how to work well with others is crucial to just about every aspect of life. But it means you have to trust other people. A great way to show people that you trust them is to constantly remind them that you all have to work together.

Allow your coworkers to carry their end of a project without you feeling the need to control it. Micromanaging your coworkers really communicates that you don't believe they can succeed. But when your words and actions continue to show everyone that you support and believe in them, it will help you accomplish the overall goal.

Your colleagues want to know that you value them and their ideas. Be compassionate toward them when they have an idea or thought with which you don't agree. You'll go a lot further by creating a culture of unity than a culture of division.

After all, this is what Jesus designed. He created us to walk in community and relationship with others. Because of Jesus, you have a unique ability to include people and form a bond over a common goal.

## Prayer

*God, would you show me the ways in which I'm not a good team player? I don't want to be the person on the team who's difficult to work with. I desire to remind people how important it is that we work together. I want the words in Hebrews 10:24 to be true of me. I want to spur others on toward love and good deeds. I know that I fall short far more than I would like. I'm asking for you to continue to work on my heart and attitude in this area. Amen.*

## Prompt

In what area of your life are you currently relying on other people to get something done? Do you find yourself getting frustrated and wanting to take all of it on yourself? If so, find one thing you can release back to the group. As you release it, find ways to speak words of unity over the people you are working with.

# Make Your Desk the Place Where Workplace Gossip Dead-Ends

*Do not let any unwholesome talk come out of your mouths, but only what is helpful for building others up according to their needs, that it may benefit those who listen.*

Ephesians 4:29, New International Version

Gossip has a way of penetrating every area of life. It often seems harmless, even though we know we shouldn't do it. That's why we need to be reminded again and again not to let any unwholesome talk come out of our mouths. In Ephesians, Paul encourages us with what *should* come from our mouths: words that are helpful in building others up. Our words should be beneficial rather than harmful or hurtful.

Whatever your work setting, it's incredibly tempting to engage in unkind conversations about the boss or whomever is in a position of leadership. And that's because it's always easier to sit on the sidelines and express how you would do things differently than it is to actually do something meaningful. The problem is that your gossip isn't beneficial to anyone.

Tamara and Dale were recently meeting with their small group at church, and one of the members pointed out that he struggles with gossip at work. This immediately hit home for Tamara. She quickly realized that people were way too comfortable sharing gossip with her about their colleagues and that this was a problem. It said a lot more about her than it did about the gossipers; it showed that she was okay with it and supported it.

As small and harmless as gossip feels in the moment, it can be destructive. It can destroy relationships in ways that are difficult to repair. To hear someone speaking ill of you is painful, and speaking ill of someone is the opposite of showing them love and compassion.

Jesus calls his people to something so much greater. He calls us to be for the good and benefit of others. Always seek to avoid contributing to the pain and hurt others experience in life.

## Prayer

*Father, forgive me for the words I have spoken against the people you love. I know how destructive it is to be spoken against, and I don't want to contribute to anyone's pain in that way. Would you help me avoid getting caught up in group gossip and help me actively hold my tongue? I don't want to speak a word about anyone that does not build up or help others. Please help me build a spirit of discipline in this area. Amen.*

## Prompt

Not only should we not gossip about others, but we also shouldn't encourage gossip, either. The next time a colleague is talking with you and begins to gossip about another person, try to find a way to end it. You can steer the conversation in a different direction, or you can explain to that person that you don't want to speak ill of anyone.

## COMPASSION
## BURNOUT TIP

It doesn't always seem possible to be intentional about compassion in the workplace. In these moments, remember that your responsibility is your role at your organization. You have to be mindful of when you're in danger of extending "compassion" at the expense of the mission of that organization.

You won't be able to cater to everyone's different emotions and personalities in every single situation, and you won't be able to bend every rule for someone else's benefit. As you extend compassion, focus still on carrying out the job that's expected of you and grant yourself grace in the midst of it.

# Find Ways to Help Team Members Get Better

*And we urge you, brothers and sisters, warn those who are idle and disruptive, encourage the disheartened, help the weak, be patient with everyone.*

1 Thessalonians 5:14, New International Version

Dale has often worked in jobs that require creativity, such as marketing, design, and social media. In these positions, where evaluating the quality of his work is a somewhat subjective process, he has thrived on honest feedback from a number of different coworkers and friends. But although he enjoys positive feedback, when he senses that people aren't willing to tell him the truth, it makes him feel uncertain about how best to move forward.

We often hear that Christians ought to love one another and always be compassionate. But too often, we think this idea means that Christians should always be "nice," and that's just not true. Sometimes, the most compassionate thing you can do is tell someone the truth. It's far easier to tell people what they want to hear or refuse to get involved. When you do that, however, you're communicating that you don't care enough to help your coworkers get better.

As Paul instructs the church in Thessalonica, being loving means tailoring our interactions with other people to what they currently need. If they're doing poorly, we need to tell them. Sometimes, people need a hard warning to improve. On the other hand, if they're feeling discouraged, we need to encourage them; if they need help, we should rise to meet their needs; and while dealing with all those circumstances, we need to be patient and humble through it all. Our hearts should desire to help others be the best they can be.

Sometimes, this means stepping into uncomfortable conversations that you would naturally want to avoid. But lean in, nonetheless, because you care enough about your colleagues to be honest.

## Prayer

*God, help me find opportunities to step into the discomfort of helping my coworkers become the best they can be. Give me the strength to be kind, honest, and loving, and keep my motives pure. May I be used to speak wisdom into the lives of those I work with. Amen.*

## Prompt

This week, pay attention to uncomfortable situations that you want to pull away from and avoid rather than leaning in and expressing honesty. Don't speak out of turn or be rude, but find a loving way to wade into discomfort for the sake of helping your coworkers.

# Go Beyond Your Job Description to Help a Coworker in a Bind

*Do not withhold good from those to whom it is due, when it is in your power to act.*

Proverbs 3:27, New International Version

When you have a job to do, it's easy to fall into the trap of only doing what's required of you. And while you might believe that you consistently outperform your coworkers, resist the urge to pat yourself on the back. You have more than a job; you have a calling. As you walk into your workplace, you are walking into an opportunity to help the organization accomplish its goals, regardless of your official job description.

In the wisdom of Proverbs, we learn that our calling is to never withhold any good thing from someone who needs it, so long as it is within our power to do so. Take this mindset with you to work. While you shouldn't unnecessarily exhaust yourself trying to do *everyone's* job, you should look for ways to help your colleagues. Even if it falls outside the purview of your job description. Even if it means you have to stay late. Even if it's terribly inconvenient and your coworker is coming to you for help on a Friday afternoon.

If you see a coworker who could use a hand with a task or project and it is within your ability to do so, rise to that calling. And don't do it because you want to look good or think it might earn you a promotion. In fact, we encourage you not to take any credit at all. Compassion isn't self-serving. Truly seek the good of your coworkers when they need a helping hand because you want them to succeed.

## Prayer

*God, help me see my job as a place where I can fulfill my calling to do good for others. Keep me from getting caught up in what my job description is or what I'm getting paid to do. Fill my heart with generosity—generosity of time and of effort. Give me eyes to see opportunities where I can go above and beyond to help my coworkers. Amen.*

## Prompt

Think back to the last time you went above and beyond your job description for the sake of helping a coworker. How long ago was it? Did you do it because you wanted to be recognized? Now, look for an opportunity this week to go outside your job description for someone. Whether it's a menial task or an important part of a large project, look to see how you might be able to ease the load of a coworker this week.

# Self-Awareness and Compassion in the Workplace

*The wisdom of the prudent is to give thought to their ways, but the folly of fools is deception.*

Proverbs 14:8, New International Version

Your ability to effectively show compassion to others is directly tied to your ability to be self-aware. We often assume that people judge us according to the intentions in our hearts, which, for the most part, are good. But our coworkers don't know our intentions. They only see the way we act and are coming across. When your intentions are misaligned with others' perception of your actions, you may be causing frustration to your coworkers without realizing it. Dale, for example, likes to think of himself as good-natured and laid-back. And, for the most part, he is. But there are times when his words are stronger or harsher than he realizes.

That's why Solomon tells us that it's wise to give thought to our actions. If you fail to stop and think about how your words and actions are affecting those with whom you work, then you might deceive yourself into thinking that you're far more kind, likeable, and compassionate than you really are. And that can hurt the relationships you have with your peers and the people you report to as well as those who report to you. What's more, it can actually keep the organization from getting necessary tasks done as your colleagues attempt to work around you.

No one wants to contribute to a difficult work environment. And yet, so many of us often do. If your workplace culture has some issues, don't assume that somebody else is the problem. Be humble enough to consider the ways that you need to increase your self-awareness so that you can be more compassionate.

## Prayer

*God, help me consider my ways. Help me pay attention to people and listen to them. Equip me to not only hear their words but to feel the heart and the emotions behind them. Allow me to see myself as I really am, and empower me to love others better in light of that reality. Amen.*

## Prompt

Sometime within the next week, approach a coworker whose judgment you trust and ask them how you really come across in the workplace. What kind of presence do you bring with you when you enter the room? What are your blind spots or the things you do unconsciously that make work harder for others? What are your best qualities that you should continue to cultivate? Be ready to have your feelings hurt and don't get defensive. Listen intently. Take note of everything they said as you observe yourself in the days following your conversation. Make adjustments where necessary to better allow yourself to display compassion to your coworkers.

# Give Your Colleagues Credit and Be Their Biggest Fan

*Let us not become conceited, provoking and envying each other.*

Galatians 5:26, New International Version

The workplace is often a site of competition, and there are times when that can certainly be healthy. Dale has always had a competitiveness to his personality. He genuinely wants to be the best. He wants to meet the deadline before his coworkers. He wants to come up with the best idea in the team meeting. Seeing his coworkers excel motivates him to work harder to rise to their level.

Many of these impulses can be incredibly positive in a work environment, causing everyone to always continue improving. But workplace competition can also contribute to a toxic work culture if you let it. When you begin to form your identity around being recognized as the best worker in your organization (or in your field for that matter), there's a very real danger that you'll begin thinking entirely too much of yourself, which will keep you from celebrating the victories of your coworkers.

That's why Paul instructs the Christians in Galatia to do everything they can to keep themselves from becoming conceited and arrogant. When you have an insatiable desire to be number one, it's really an indication that your pride has gotten out of hand. Pride makes you see others purely as your competition—your enemies—and it leads you to provoke them into conflict. You don't just want to be the best you can be; you want to beat them.

If you find yourself falling prey to this kind of prideful and selfish mindset, here's an important countermeasure you can take: begin celebrating your coworkers every time they experience a win. Instead of being jealous, choose to be genuinely happy for them. Cheer them on. Be their biggest supporter. It might not come naturally, but it's important to remind yourself that their success doesn't mean your failure. Refuse to see them as your enemy. Instead, see them as a friend who works just as hard as you do and who genuinely deserves to succeed.

## Prayer

*Father God, keep me from becoming prideful and toxically competitive with my coworkers. When they experience a win, make me genuinely happy for them. Keep me from resenting them or feeling jealous. Let my support for them be genuine. Amen.*

## Prompt

The next time a coworker experiences a win over and above what you were able to accomplish on a project, take a moment to consider how you're feeling. What emotions are naturally welling up within you? If you're feeling anger, insecurity, or frustration, say a prayer to help shift your focus. Then, encourage and congratulate your coworker. Be as genuine about it as you possibly can.

# Assume You Don't Know the Whole Story

*Many are the plans in the mind of a man, but it is the purpose of the Lord that will stand.*

Proverbs 19:21, English Standard Version

Workplace bottlenecks can be so frustrating, especially when you feel perpetually hindered by a coworker who isn't doing what needs to be done so that you can complete your job duties. We don't always know the whole story behind why someone let you down at work. The real issue is often our expectations: we have plans set in our mind that we want to follow through until the end, but it doesn't always happen that way. Proverbs 19:21 tells us that we can plan all we want but it's ultimately God's plans that prevail.

You don't get to control everything, even though you'd probably like to, and that means you can't control the outcomes of other people's work. Sometimes, those outcomes are out of their control as well.

It's important to see situations in which a coworker has disappointed you or let you down as opportunities to learn the whole story. You might see a missed deadline as evidence that your coworker is lazy or unorganized, but it's likely that there's more to it than that. Maybe they're currently dealing with a difficult family situation, or perhaps they're simply feeling overwhelmed by other tasks at work.

When situations like this come about, instead of being upset about your plans being ruined, extend compassion toward your coworker. It's far better to assume that you don't know the full story than to react with partial information.

Care for your coworkers, even when you feel inconvenienced. Your compassion and grace toward your colleague in an unfortunate situation will go a long way in showing the love of Jesus flowing in you. Tasks and responsibilities are important, but caring for people is far more important.

## Prayer

*Lord, I acknowledge that I don't always know the full story and I'm often too quick to respond with limited information. Would you give me the mindfulness to extend grace before frustration and judgment? I want to be known for keeping an open mind and giving others the benefit of the doubt rather than reacting emotionally. I need you to keep me mindful and compassionate toward others. Amen.*

## Prompt

This week, you will likely face a frustrating or inconvenient scenario. In that moment, stop and think through how you plan to respond. Allow that response to be filled with grace. Hold off on responding until you are in a place to extend grace.

# THE BENEFITS
# OF COMPASSION

If you're in a position of leadership at your workplace, or if you want to be in one someday, compassion is key in increasing your leadership capacity. If you are able to play a role in fostering a culture of compassion, you'll become a valuable asset to your organization, and you'll contribute in very meaningful ways to its success. That's because compassion allows you to gain influence in the lives and work of others.

When people feel cared for, they are willing to do more, try harder, and give their best effort. This isn't some kind of emotional manipulation or quid pro quo. If you sincerely care for others, they will naturally want to contribute to your success. When you make your coworkers feel like you'd do anything for them, they'll likely do anything for you.

Showing compassion in your workplace is the right thing to do, but it's also a smart habit to form. Paul gives this encouragement to the church in Rome in Romans 14:19 (New International Version):

*"Let us therefore make every effort to do what leads to peace and to mutual edification."*

When you seek to build others up, you'll end up being built up yourself. When you take care of those around you, it's far more likely that they'll go out of their way to return the favor.

## CHAPTER FOUR

# LOCAL COMMUNITY

**It may be difficult** to fully comprehend the idea of God walking among us, but that's exactly who Jesus was. What's even more striking is that Jesus didn't reign over the people from an ivory tower. He came to be with them and among them, living where they lived, eating where they ate, and spending his time where the people could be found. Jesus prioritized his local community. In fact, during his three-year ministry, he never left the borders of Israel.

A sense of community is embedded into Jesus's story. During the course of his life, Jesus attended weddings (John 2:1–12), comforted families who had suffered the loss of a loved one (Mark 5:36–43), went to parties (Luke 14:1), went to worship services at the synagogue (Luke 4:31–37), and spent time in community gathering places (John 4:4–6). In each of these community settings, Jesus brought the very presence of God with him, blessing everyone with whom he came into contact.

When Jesus was among us, he gave us an example of the life-transforming presence he wanted his people to have. And after he rose from the dead, just before he ascended into heaven, he imparted to his followers an incredible calling: to change the world.

As big a calling as that is, Jesus didn't tell his followers to immediately pack their bags and travel to distant places in his name, though that's eventually what they did. Before they could get there, Jesus wanted them to transform the community in which they lived.

This is what he said to them in Acts 1:8 (New International Version):

*"But you will receive power when the Holy Spirit comes on you; and you will be my witnesses in Jerusalem, and in all Judea and Samaria, and to the ends of the earth."*

The calling to change the world began in Jerusalem, where the disciples were staying. It then expanded to the surrounding community of Judea, where the city of Jerusalem was located, and then to the adjacent community of Samaria. Only after all those local areas had been reached did their mission expand to the ends of the earth. Our first call is to our local community.

If you have given your life to Jesus, he has given you his in return. The Holy Spirit is an ever-present companion in your life. And whenever you enter into a community setting, you bring the presence of God with you, which means that you have the very same power that Jesus had to bless everyone with whom you come into contact.

In this chapter, we'll explore how to be a transformative force for compassion in your local community, whether you live in a large city or a small town. As you consider the prompts, try to think of the specific names and faces of the people in your community: your neighbors and acquaintances, local business owners, and community officials. How do you want to be a part of bringing transformation to their lives individually and collectively?

# Be for the Good of Your City

*Also, seek the peace and prosperity of the city to which
I have carried you into exile. Pray to the Lord for it,
because if it prospers, you too will prosper.*

Jeremiah 29:7, New International Version

About 600 years before the birth of Jesus, something terrible
happened to the people of Israel. They were conquered by a
foreign invader and led into an exile that would last 70 years.
During the first years of their captivity, a number of prophets
in the community encouraged the people that they wouldn't
be away from their home for very long.

Jeremiah had a different message. The people were going
to be there for longer than they thought. They weren't going
back to their homeland anytime soon, but that didn't need to
be entirely bad. Although many aspects of the future seemed
uncertain, they could have a part in bringing about good
things to the city in which they found themselves. In fact, if
they sought the good of their city, the people of Israel would
prosper, too. So, if they wanted a better life for their kids,
then it was best for them to invest in their city, even if they
didn't *feel* like it was their city.

Dale has often felt like it's been difficult to really invest
in the community. That might be because he's seen a
number of major life transitions in the last few years,
whether a job change, graduating school, getting married,
moving, or having a baby. It's hard to get motivated to
invest in your community if you always feel like you're just
passing through.

So, let us encourage you with this. Regardless of how long
you've been in your community, or how long you think you

might be there, be committed to investing in it. Pursue the good of your city.

Seek to understand the needs of your community. Listen to what community leaders—whether they are city leaders, pastors, or even influential business owners—talk about and what's important to them. Find ways to invest in what's important to your city. If you do, you might get just as much out of it as you meant to give.

## Prayer

*God, give me a heart for my city and my community. Help me see, understand, and care about what's important to the people of my city. Motivate me to invest in the people around me in new ways, regardless of how long I've been here or how long I think I'm going to be here. Amen.*

## Prompt

Make a list of the things you think are important to your city. What are your community's values? What are its needs? Are there programs that are seeking to build into those values and meet those needs? Do some research. If you have access to a community leader and are able to meet with them, ask them what you can do to invest in the community.

# Empathize with the Hurt of People Who Don't Look like You

*But a Samaritan, as he traveled, came where the man was; and when he saw him, he took pity on him.*

Luke 10:33, New International Version

It's easiest to be compassionate to the people who look like us or are close to us—people whose values and experiences closely align with our own. But the beauty of true compassion is that it moves beyond those boundaries.

Jesus once told a parable about a man who was attacked by bandits while traveling. He was robbed, beaten, and left for dead. As he lay in the road, two separate religious leaders passed him by, not wanting to get involved or risk being attacked themselves.

Then came a Samaritan man. Now, Samaritans were not well liked or respected by the Jewish people because they were racially mixed and their beliefs about God brought together various Jewish teachings but united them with other religious values.

None of these differences mattered to the Samaritan man. He saw someone in need, and he had compassion for him. He picked him up, tended to his wounds, and brought him to an inn to be cared for. He saved his life—the life of a man who might not have respected him or even given him a moment of attention if he encountered him any other way. This is the level of compassion for your community to which Jesus is calling you. It's a kind of compassion that tears down the walls that divide us.

We're almost never intentional about it, but when we're involved in initiatives to care for the community, we're most likely to be involved in the initiatives that benefit people just like us. It's not until you see the needs of those that don't look like you that you'll be able to rise to meet them. So, begin to look. You'll be amazed at the opportunities you'll find.

## Prayer

*Father God, give me eyes to see the needs of people who are different from me—people who have different backgrounds and experiences from me. Don't let me fall into a prejudice of passivity, but activate me to tangibly love people across lines of race, ethnicity, socioeconomic status, cultural values, and religion. May it all be a testimony of the kind of love you offer through Jesus. Amen.*

## Prompt

Take inventory of all the community initiatives you contribute to, whether financially or through volunteering your time. Who benefits most from those initiatives? Is it those who look most like you? If that's the case, consider reallocating a portion of your time and resources to a community initiative that helps people who look nothing like you.

# Make Your Local Church a Priority

*All the believers were one in heart and mind. No one
claimed that any of their possessions was their own,
but they shared everything they had.*

Acts 4:32, New International Version

In the early days of the Church, believers often contended
with the fact that the world was, quite literally, against them.
When they came to faith in Jesus, their family and friends
might disassociate from them, and they often faced per-
secution from government leaders. And yet, the number of
believers among them continued to grow.

That's because Jesus had given the Church such a singu-
lar purpose and sense of hope that they became one in heart
and mind. In the early days of the Church, there was no one
among them in need because they cared for one another
that well both through relationships and by pooling their
resources. So, if you want to learn about compassion in the
context of community, the Church is uniquely equipped to
teach you.

To bring compassion to your community, it's important to
leverage the most important resource you have: your local
church. The Church is unique among all other organizations
in that it is the place where the Spirit of Jesus dwells. So, your
church wields supernatural power and authority as it seeks
to be a transformative agent in the community.

This isn't to say the Church is perfect. If you're anything like us, you've often been frustrated when you
feel the Church isn't moving quickly enough to meet the

community's needs. But that's why they need *you*. You have unique gifts and passions that will help your church be as compassionate as it was meant to be. If God has placed a burden on your heart for your community, the best way to tackle it is alongside your fellow followers of Jesus.

## Prayer

*God, show me the power and authority you have uniquely given to the Church. Show me how I can support my pastors and church in bringing about acts of compassion in the community. Rather than simply expecting the church leaders to do it, show me how I can get involved to express your love to my community. Amen.*

## Prompt

Are you consistently involved in your church's efforts to extend compassion to the community? If your church doesn't have a specific plan for showing compassion in your city, then consider drafting a proposal for how it might form one. Be patient with your pastors and church leaders, and be respectful of them. Form a plan about how you might come under their leadership and help them do something that they're probably already passionate about but haven't been able to have the church carry out as a group.

# Be a Voice of Unity in Divisive Times

*How good and pleasant it is when God's people live together in unity!*

Psalm 133:1, New International Version

We live in very divisive times. From cable news to social media channels, our public platforms are often a place where people vent their anger, frustrations, and pointed opinions. There are key issues that serve to divide us across political, racial, and cultural lines.

It's so important for followers of Jesus to create a counter-culture of unity through compassion in the age of social media divisiveness. This isn't to say that Christians should ignore important issues, but they must approach them through the lens of compassion and self-sacrifice. Dale often struggles to know when to "speak truth" on controversial topics. After all, which parts of his views on a given topic are absolute truth, and which are matters of opinion? As you wrestle with that question, you'll become a more effective agent of unity.

There's something so healing to be in the presence of someone who's more interested in loving the person standing in front of them than in winning a particular argument. When you're in a community where that's the culture, it becomes a place where everyone wants to be.

David writes in Psalm 133 that it's good and pleasant when the people of God live in unity. Later in this psalm, he compares a spirit of unity to precious oil and lush grass. In David's time, oil was a rare and expensive luxury that moisturized skin and hair, and wet grass was a sign that there was moisture in the air. In an agrarian society that counted on crops to survive, rainwater was a symbol for life itself. So, when David uses these similes, he's saying that unity has restorative power that fills us back up with life.

You have the opportunity to model this kind of compassion in your community. As you interact with the other members of your community, find ways to establish common ground with opposing parties. Be an advocate for empathy.

## Prayer

*Father God, keep me from becoming a divisive person. Help me bring unity through compassion. May I be known as a person who is good and pleasant to be around because I'm more concerned with loving the person in front of me than winning an argument. May my compassion be contagious, and may it lead to greater amounts of unity. Amen.*

## Prompt

Take inventory of your social media feed. How much of what you're posting is divisive? How much is uplifting and encouraging? Take the same inventory with your text messages and emails. What is the general tenor of your conversations? If you find yourself being negative and divisive, remind yourself to enter into every conversation looking for common ground. Encourage those close to you to do the same.

# Pray for the Needs of Your Community

*For this reason, since the day we heard about you, we have not stopped praying for you. We continually ask God to fill you with the knowledge of his will through all the wisdom and understanding that the Spirit gives.*

*Colossians 1:9, New International Version*

Dale tends to have a bias for action. Whenever he hears about a problem, his immediate instinct is to develop a plan: to research the issue, to contact someone who might be able to help, to create action steps for moving forward. This instinct has often led to actionable solutions. In the midst of that, however, Dale too often treats prayer like an afterthought, almost as if it serves as a rubber stamp of approval on his best-laid plans.

But prayer is actually essential to compassion. The Apostle Paul knew that better than anybody.

Paul had preached great sermons and performed miracles that transformed people's lives. He had written letters that are still read as divinely authoritative almost 2,000 years later. Perhaps the most compassionate thing Paul did for the people he led was that he always seemed to be praying for them. In every one of Paul's letters, we find a large section devoted to speaking about how he was praying for the people he was writing to. As he writes to the Christians in Colossae, he prays that God would fill them with wisdom and spiritual understanding.

Prayer is powerful. It leads to change. When you invite God into the situation, you're calling on the infinite Creator of the universe who cares about the problems of your community far more than you ever could. When you invite his power to meet the needs of your community, that's when you can really make an impact.

You might feel like you're not doing anything until you spring into action. But it's important to remember that, when you're on your knees, you're changing the world.

## Prayer

*God, give me a very real belief in the power of prayer. More than something I know I'm supposed to do, make prayer something that I want to do. Allow me to experience the power that comes from inviting you into a situation. Open my eyes to everything you are doing around me. Amen.*

## Prompt

Schedule time in your daily calendar to meet with God and pray for your community. What are the needs of your neighborhood, city, and region? How do you want to see God move? Write out some of your prayers. This will give you focus, and it will provide a record for you to revisit and reflect on the ways God is answering your prayers.

## SELF-COMPASSION TIP

We all want to think of ourselves as compassionate people, but every once in a while, someone might call you out on an area of your life where compassion is lacking. That can be painful, but we encourage you to receive what that person has said to you (or even about you).

Pay attention to the valid points they've made, but don't dwell on them. You don't have to relive the mistakes you've made, every day or every time you encounter a similar situation. Understand what caused you to respond the way you did and build from there.

# Open Your Life to Others

*Jesus replied, "You must love the Lord your God with all your heart, all your soul, and all your mind." This is the first and greatest commandment. A second is equally important: "Love your neighbor as yourself."*

*Matthew 22:37–39, New Living Translation*

These might be the most well-known words of Jesus. The religious leaders of the time were asking him what the most important command to keep was, and this was his response. This is the key to fulfilling everything Jesus is calling you to: love God and other people. His answer is so often recited that Christians and non-Christians alike are aware of the call to love their neighbor.

As you seek to fulfill the call to genuinely love the members of your community, one important way to do that is simply to open your life to them. Make space in your life with them in mind. That means adding room in your schedule, in your emotional and mental capacity, and even in your physical spaces.

When you're functioning at full capacity—or even beyond capacity—it can feel like there's no margin to allow the messiness of other people into your life. But although you can't fulfill every single need, Jesus is calling you to be intentional about making space to love your neighbors. When you're rushing to get inside your house or to your next obligation, opportunities to take the time to chat and get to know your neighbors are almost nonexistent. This has to change. In order to cultivate more meaningful relationships, you need to pack your life with a little less.

Creating intentional space isn't an easy task in our 24/7 world, but it's an important adjustment you might need to make. When you have a little more space in your day, you will discover more opportunities to engage with other people.

## Prayer

*Heavenly Father, I need to make more space in my life to love others. I need to make more space to show your love to my community. Would you show me the tasks or commitments that I can let go of? I want to have time for people. Help me be more about engaging with people and less about doing things. I need your clarity and wisdom in this area of my life. Amen.*

## Prompt

Look at what's taking up space in your life, whether mentally, physically, and emotionally. What's one thing you can "unload" to make space for the well-being of others? It might only be a 20-minute space, but that's a great start. Take this time to free up some of your schedule and use it to engage with one of your neighbors.

# Speak Prophetically to Build Up Your Community

*Better is open rebuke than hidden love. Wounds from a friend can be trusted, but an enemy multiplies kisses.*

Proverbs 27:5–6, New International Version

No one enjoys being rebuked. But when someone is willing to lovingly share about your faults in the context of a relationship, you can know that there is an established trust. This proverb expresses the importance of being willing to offer correction and rebuke when necessary. As a member of your community, being aware of the areas where it should be nurtured to grow is vital.

If you see an injustice or an oversight within your community, you have a responsibility to speak rebuke and correction. In areas of injustice or insensitivity, you can bring light and compassion. When those who are weak and marginalized feel as if they have no voice, you have an opportunity to use your voice for them. There is no place that you can have a greater impact in these areas than in your own local community.

This is about more than seeing the wrong. It's about speaking into it and being part of the change toward what Jesus has called you to. Healing and rebuilding can begin when you decide to take the hard step forward and point out the wrong. Only when someone sheds light on the dark areas can restoration begin, so you need to be aware of what is happening in your community. Consider the groups you gather with in your neighborhood, your city, or even your county.

Sometimes, actively seeking compassion will require you to make difficult decisions that others will dislike. In the Old Testament, prophets were called to bring the sins of Israel to light and encourage them to repent. This wasn't for the sake of calling people out; it was for their healing and rebuilding. The same can be true in your communities. As you see any injustice or sin within your community that is commonly accepted, you need to speak against it. And no matter how many people might oppose you, rest assured that God will be with you.

## Prayer

*Lord, open my eyes to the overlooked needs and injustices happening in my community. Raise up a spirit within me to reject these things. Give me the voice to speak to those I must and take action where you see fit. I don't want to sit in a community that is accepting injustices and mistreatment of fellow people who are created in your image. Amen.*

## Prompt

What areas of needed improvement have you recognized in your community? If you think there are none, pray daily throughout this week for God to open your eyes to what you may not have seen. If you are aware of something, what is one action step you can take to bringing about change?

# Get to Know Your Neighbors

*And Jonathan made a solemn pact with David, because he loved him as he loved himself.*

1 Samuel 18:3, New Living Translation

The friendship of David and Jonathan is noteworthy for many reasons. Jonathan was the son of King Saul, who later does everything in his power to try to kill David. Yet, Jonathan remains a faithful and trustworthy friend to David in spite of his father's views. The reason Jonathan continues to love David as himself is because he *knew* David. He knew that David was a good man and that the hate Saul had for him was unmerited.

In order to have the kind of compassion and love for people that you have for yourself, you need to know them. It has been said this way: proximity brings forth empathy. It's really hard to understand where someone is coming from if you've never really known them. There's a bridge that is built between you and a stranger even by simply knowing their name—a connection that wasn't there before.

Tamara recently heard about a terrible car accident that claimed the lives of three young boys. She was troubled by it, but the report sat differently when she realized that she knew the mother of one of those boys. She didn't know the mother well, but she remembered a few passing conversations she'd had with her at church. In that moment, Tamara felt the weight of the deaths reported in the news. She felt deep compassion for this acquaintance. So, she reached out to see if there was any way she could help or offer support.

Hearing about a tragedy or hardship in your local community impacts you differently when you know the person involved. If you get to know the people in your community, you have the opportunity to extend compassion and support in times of need. This may sound simple, but in order to love others, we have to know them.

## Prayer

*Lord, give me a heart for your people. I want to know the people in my community personally. Would you give me opportunities to get to know them? I hope for people to know me as the neighbor who cared rather than the one who kept to themselves. Amen.*

## Prompt

Do you know the names of the people who live within an eight-door radius of you? If you don't, be intentional this week about learning their names. This might mean you need to leave your garage door open a little longer or that you should look for opportunities to be outside more rather than rushing into your house.

# Be Hospitable

*Rather, [a church leader] must enjoy having guests in his home, and he must love what is good. He must live wisely and be just. He must live a devout and disciplined life.*

Titus 1:8, New Living Translation

You might not be a leader in your church, but you are likely a leader in *some* way. That's because leadership is simply having influence in the lives of others. You might be a leader in your home, at work, or in your community, and one of the characteristics of a leader is having the willingness and confidence to open your home to your community. An open home is a sign of an open heart and a hospitable spirit.

As a member of your local community, opening your home is a wonderful opportunity to show love in action to those around you. It doesn't mean you have to cook an elaborate meal or have the latest forms of entertainment. Inviting people into your home allows them to lower their guard and enter into your personal space so that they can get to know you more deeply. Many great relationships have been built around kitchen tables and living room floors.

You might have fears of inviting people into your home, but allowing those fears to win lets the enemy rob you of an opportunity to know and love others in your community. It's in this place of vulnerability and sacrifice that God will work. We often view our homes as personal sanctuaries to drown out the rest of the world, but God invites us to use our homes as a place of ministry. Your home is a gift from God, no matter how big or small. It's a resource you have been given—an opportunity to use what you have for the glory of God.

This gift you have been given is a tool to show people in your community that you truly care for them and desire to show them compassion. People tend to open up and be honest when they feel welcome and secure. Your home is the perfect setting to foster beautiful relationships.

## Prayer

*God, thank you for the home you have given me. I want to use it as a resource to display your glory rather than a place for me to hide away. Would you help me move past my fears and insecurities or any other thing that's holding me back? I want people to come into my home and feel your love. Show me how to love my community through my home. Amen.*

## Prompt

Think of a neighbor you can invite over. In the next two days, select a date and invite that person into your home. Think of how you can make them feel completely welcome in your home. What are some ways that you can use your home to build trust and intimacy with your community?

# Be Willing to Share
# Your Story

*And I want you to know, my dear brothers and sisters,*
*that everything that has happened to me here has*
*helped to spread the Good News.*

Philippians 1:12, New Living Translation

One of the most encouraging letters in the New Testament is to the church in Philippi, which, surprisingly, Paul wrote when he was in prison. There wasn't one good or bad situation in Paul's life that God didn't use to spread the good news about Jesus. Even when he was in prison, he was proclaiming that the situation would be used for the glory of God.

God can use every moment in your life for his glory. Your story of how Jesus has worked in your life is important, and it needs to be told. The people in your community need to know your story. It's through sharing your story that walls are broken down and people become open to hearing about Jesus. There's power in your story, whether you think so or not. As you continue to build relationships in your community, others should know about what is most important to you. They should know about Jesus.

Certainly, the opportunity to share about your faith won't always present itself immediately, and you should be mindful of the receptiveness of the person to whom you're talking. But the people in your community should know that you're a follower of Jesus not only by how you act but by the things you share. If Jesus truly is the center of your heart and life, then you can't help but share. Don't shy away from discussing the ugly details of your life. Tamara and Dale have experienced a number of hardships and made a myriad of poor choices in life, and God has used it all. So, don't be afraid to share it all with someone.

You have no control over how another person will respond, but that fear shouldn't hinder you from sharing anyway. The hope you have is one of salvation and freedom for all who believe. Jesus truly desires for all to be saved. Extending compassion to your community means caring for the state of other people's souls. Jesus is the only one who can save, but he can use you and your story in that process.

## Prayer

*God, would you use my story to share your good news? I want people to know who you are when they encounter me. I don't want simply to be a good neighbor who's hospitable and kind but who never cares enough to share Jesus. There are moments when it's scary, but I ask that your Spirit would work in me and help me push past my fears. Amen.*

## Prompt

Do you have a neighbor you know well who doesn't know that you're a Christian? Pray for God to prompt you in your upcoming conversations to share your story. What are some brave and vulnerable ways you could share your story with them? God will present opportunities if you are willing and aware.

## THE BENEFITS
## OF COMPASSION

Everyone longs to be a part of something bigger than themselves—to have a sense of belonging, meaning, and collective purpose. Many of us continue to wait for someone to invite us into this kind of community, but we often fail to realize that we don't actually have to wait to be asked. We have the power to create it ourselves. If you want to be included, create an inclusive space for others. If you want to be heard, learn to listen.

Jesus talks about this in his Sermon on the Mount in an often quoted verse, Matthew 7:12 (New International Version):

*"Do to others what you would have them do to you."*

We're called to uphold this principle even when the receiving party doesn't reciprocate. But what's amazing is that, more often than not, they will. When you build into the local community, the local community builds into you.

So, rather than being discouraged, feel a great sense of empowerment when you notice a lack of community in your life. Many of the benefits you wish to receive are available to you if you are willing to give them selflessly to others. When you cultivate a compassionate, community-building mindset, there are so many people who long to experience all the same things you want to receive from your community. They were just waiting for your invitation.

 CHAPTER FIVE

# GLOBAL COMMUNITY

**When we open our** hearts to compassion for those around us, something beautiful happens. We begin to see transformation within our communities. Lives genuinely change when we're willing to listen to people's stories, feel their pain, and work together toward a better tomorrow.

And as much as we're thankful for the ways we can see God moving in our local communities and cultures, he has an even bigger vision. He's inviting us to broaden our understanding of what it looks like to live out our compassion.

God has a global vision for restoration and renewal. We should, too. And God's global vision isn't anything new. In fact, we see it way back in the life of a man named Abraham. This is the promise God made to him in Genesis 18:18 (New International Version):

*"Abraham will surely become a great and powerful nation, and all nations on earth will be blessed through him."*

God promised to turn Abraham's descendants into a great nation that would bless him and give him an enduring legacy, but that promise came with a purpose. Through that one nation that would come from Abraham, all the nations of the world would experience blessing.

This promise was eventually fulfilled by Jesus.

The point is that Abraham was blessed in order to be a blessing—and not only within his own tribe and community, but to the entire world for generations to come. This is the kind of vision we need to capture and commit to. When it comes to compassion, maybe it's time to think bigger than we ever have before.

We have access to news from around the world at our fingertips. And because of that, it's easy to get discouraged by how much need we see around the world. Problems such as lack of food and clean water, lack of access to medical care and social welfare infrastructures, oppression, and economic injustice run rampant in many parts of the world—so much so that it's difficult to know where to start.

It's easy for us to distance ourselves from that pain because we're separated from it by things like geography, culture, religion, and socioeconomic status. We often use those things to shield us from experiencing the pain of others because, if we allowed it to, the sheer depth and breadth of need would overwhelm us.

But you can't let that be a reason for inaction. Instead, let it inspire you to begin imagining a world where these needs are being met. Although you won't be able to meet every single need, you can start doing *something*.

So, begin opening your heart to the global need for compassion. Allow yourself to feel the pain of your fellow human beings around the world and find something helpful you can do.

If enough of us begin to do that, we will see change on a scale that we could never have imagined. This is what you were meant to do. You are blessed to be a blessing.

# Living in Harmony

*After this I looked, and there before me was a great multitude that no one could count, from every nation, tribe, people and language, standing before the throne and before the Lamb.*

Revelation 7:9, New International Version

In order to capture a global sense of compassion, we first need to realize that a restored world will be marked by unity amid diversity of culture, race, and ethnicity.

In Revelation, the Apostle John is given a glimpse of heaven. In this vision, he sees a crowd of people too large to count, all diverse in their appearance and values but unified in song and heart. This is just a glimpse of what the heart of God looks like.

The world as we know it is full of great diversity. Heaven will be no different because Jesus came to offer salvation to the entire world. Though the tribes living deep in the Amazon rainforest may feel worlds apart from you, they are still made in the image of God just as you are.

Many years ago, Tamara traveled to South Africa for a four-month long mission trip. She felt out of place in a culture and location that was so new to her. At first, it was difficult, but she quickly realized that the people who lived all the way on the other side of the world struggled with the same innate desire to belong—to be known and loved and accepted by others. Her heart opened toward this community. It was a truly life-changing experience.

We don't always have the opportunity to personally meet a group of people on the other side of the world. However, that doesn't mean we can't seek to understand their humanity a little better, and it certainly doesn't mean that we can't have deep compassion for them.

Every tribe, nation, and tongue is precious to Jesus. So, as we seek to be more like Jesus, they should be equally precious to us.

## Prayer

*Lord, it's easy to lack compassion for people on the other side of the world. Would you give me a heart and a love for the people you have created? Would you give me an opportunity to experience the humanity of someone from a culture that's completely foreign to me? Amen.*

## Prompt

The next time you see or hear news about a tragedy in another part of the world, try to imagine what it would be like if you were in that situation. How could you be praying for those people and the difficulty they're facing? What could you do to get involved?

# Donate Financially to Global Compassion Efforts

*For Macedonia and Achaia were pleased to make a*
*contribution for the poor among the Lord's people*
*in Jerusalem.*

Romans 15:26, New International Version

Compassion requires sacrifice. When we say that we care about something, it's important to put our money where our mouth is.

Throughout his New Testament letters, Paul constantly called upon the church communities to whom he was writing to do just that. He spoke often about one initiative in particular: a collection for the church in Jerusalem. During the early days of the church, Jerusalem had the distinction of being a hub for training new believers. But hosting so many people from out of town was a considerable financial burden, so the Jerusalem Christians had many financial needs.

In response to this need, Paul took collections from churches in various regions throughout the Roman Empire. He asked people to financially contribute to meet the needs of people they didn't know and would never meet, and those churches responded with incredible generosity. May we do the same today.

To spread compassion worldwide, you can give to any number of nonprofit efforts, whether it is a clean water initiative, an organization fighting global sex trafficking, a child sponsorship program, or some other group that's seeking to be a redemptive force by addressing the needs of the most vulnerable worldwide.

PRACTICING CHRISTIAN COMPASSION

The choices may seem a little overwhelming, and you only have so many resources to offer by way of financial contributions. Dale and Tamara sometimes feel bad that they don't have the resources to give substantial financial gifts to every organization that's doing works of compassion in the world. Our heart is sometimes bigger than our budget; maybe you feel the same way.

But don't let that move you toward inaction, and certainly don't let it move you toward feelings of guilt or inadequacy. You have resources that God has given to you and the ability to invest them in making a global impact for good.

## Prayer

*God, plant a seed of generosity in my heart and cause it to grow. Give me ambitious, worldwide dreams for how I spend my money. Help me make an impact for compassion around the world with the resources you have given me. Give me wisdom to know how best to allocate my financial contributions. Amen.*

## Prompt

What issues or problems in the world weigh heaviest on your heart? Is there an area of the world that you feel God placing on your heart? Spend some time in reflection and jot down your thoughts. Then, do some research to see if you can find any nonprofit organizations that are spearheading those global compassion efforts to which you might consider giving.

# Be a Sender

*How, then, can they call on the one they have not believed in? And how can they believe in the one of whom they have not heard? And how can they hear without someone preaching to them? And how can anyone preach unless they are sent? As it is written: "How beautiful are the feet of those who bring good news!"*

Romans 10:14–15, New International Version

One of the most important components of true compassion is sharing the good news of Jesus. It's possible to meet every physical need of a person and still miss their most important one: their need for Jesus. When we take a global perspective, we quickly see how great that need is.

That's why Paul said, in his letter to the Romans, that the feet of those who bring good news are "beautiful." In many places throughout the world, people do not have access to a local church, which means they don't even have the opportunity to hear the good news of Jesus, let alone experience the power of his redemption.

You might not be called to be a global missionary, but that doesn't mean that you can't be a part of God's global mission. Paul says that no one can preach unless they are sent. So, the role of the sender is vital to the mission of Jesus's ultimate compassion.

Your local church likely supports at least one missionary family in the field, and the money you give to your church is likely part of that support. But being a true sender involves so much more. So, find ways to support those global missionaries.

One way to support your church's missionaries is simply to commit to regularly praying for them. Missionaries are constantly battling both physical and spiritual obstacles, so they need prayer. Another way to support missionaries is by encouraging them. You can do this through letters and online communications, treating them to a coffee or a meal while they are home on furlough, or asking about what specific needs they have that you might be able to help with.

Your support will mean more than you know, and it serves as an important part of spreading the good news of Jesus together.

## Prayer

*God, help me be supportive of your global missionaries. Give me opportunities to encourage the missionaries my church supports. Put their names on my heart and show me how to be an important part of their support team, whatever that looks like. Amen.*

## Prompt

If you don't know already, find out which missionaries your local church currently supports. If possible, get their contact information and reach out to them via letter or email. Let them know you are praying for them and ask them how they might need support.

# Become a Student of Other Cultures

*To the Jews I became like a Jew, to win the Jews. To those under the law I became like one under the law (though I myself am not under the law), so as to win those under the law.*

1 Corinthians 9:20, New International Version

Having grown up in Southern California, Dale has always appreciated the cultural and ethnic diversity around him. From different foods, customs, and collective stories, his life has been enriched by having friendships with people who have a different background from him.

In a way, when we come to understand the stories of people from different cultures, we understand more of what it means to be human. All people are created in the image of God, and different cultures highlight and accentuate different aspects of God's image.

During his missionary journeys, Paul often adapted to fit into different cultures so that he might more effectively love them. When he was among Jewish people, he followed Jewish customs. When he was among non-Jews, he set his own customs aside in order to be a part of their community.

When you learn about another culture and how to love the people within it, you begin to feel their burdens and care more deeply for them. Knowing the burdens of people across cultures will give you a more global sense of compassion.

Fear—of the unknown, of doing the wrong thing, of being rejected—often keeps us from deepening relationships of compassion across cultures. Don't let fear keep you from extending compassion beyond your own culture. Reach out to those who are different from you. Seek friendships with immigrants and their children. Learn their stories. Allow God to grow your heart for them.

## Prayer

*Father God, help me extend my compassion across cultural lines. Allow me to deepen relationships with people whose stories are so different from mine. Give me opportunities to learn more about what it means to be made in your image by learning the stories of those who come from a different cultural background. Amen.*

## Prompt

Is there someone in your community who comes from a different culture? It could be a neighbor, classmate, coworker, or someone who goes to your church. What do you want to know about them? What questions do you have? The next time you see them, engage them in conversation and ask them more about themselves.

# Go on a Short-Term Mission Trip

*From Troas we put out to sea and sailed straight for*
*Samothrace, and the next day we went on to Neapolis.*

Acts 16:11, New International Version

After coming to faith in Jesus, the Apostle Paul spent most
of his time traveling from place to place, spreading the good
news of Jesus. On each journey, he took companions with
him. He employed their help and trained them in the kind
of work he was doing. In Acts 16, he set sail with Silas, Luke,
and Timothy. Each of those three men went on to serve
the church in important ways, even though not all of them
ended up living on the road quite as much as Paul did.

You might not feel called to move to remote places of the
world to engage in acts of compassion there, but you can
still find opportunities to be present in those places on a
short-term basis.

A great way to support long-term missionaries is to go on
a short-term mission trip. You can encourage someone who
lives in that region full time in order to spread the love of
Jesus, and you can act as an extra set of hands in the mission they are trying to carry out. Furthermore, once you've
spent time in the field, you can come back and champion the
cause of what that missionary is doing.

Whether it was spending time with church leaders
in Europe, aiding communities in Mexico, or rebuilding
homes damaged by hurricanes in New Orleans, Dale has
always been transformed in some way by participating in
short-term mission trips. Each new place he's gone to serve

has impacted him and expanded his understanding of the genuine needs of people who live nowhere near him.

Consider taking an opportunity to go on a short-term mission trip through your local church or another missions organization. It won't necessarily be an easy experience, but it will go a long way in helping you learn how to be a part of worldwide compassion. You might even find ways to meaningfully partner in these global efforts on a longer-term basis.

## Prayer

*God, give me an opportunity to go serve people in another region. May I have the opportunity to meet people where they are and help them in any way I can for however brief a time I might be there. Amen.*

## Prompt

Is your church offering any short-term mission trip opportunities this year? If so, prayerfully consider applying for one. Remember that a mission trip is different from a vacation and requires a significant sacrifice of resources, time, and comfort. However, if you're willing to make these sacrifices, you may find your mission trip to be a life-changing opportunity to extend compassion beyond your immediate community.

# COMPASSION BURNOUT TIP

Trying to extend compassion to the entire world is an overwhelming proposition. In a world in which you have access to far more information than you could ever act on, you might really begin to understand exactly how finite you are as an individual.

Choose only a few issues, causes, or initiatives that you want to act on. Actively pursue a couple of things that you can manage, knowing that even though you can't save the whole world, you can make a meaningful impact when you put focused effort into select compassion initiatives.

# Care for the Environment for the Sake of Others

*The Lord God took the man and put him in the Garden of Eden to work it and take care of it.*

Genesis 2:15, New International Version

When God created the world, everything was exactly the way it was supposed to be. He created everything on Earth to be good, and when he created humanity, he put us in charge of caring for every good thing he created. Right after God created Adam, he put him in the Garden of Eden to work it and care for it. As Adam cared for the land, it also cared for him by providing food and a place to live comfortably.

In our efforts to have a heart of global compassion, we mustn't neglect the earth itself. God has given us the planet as a resource; the better we care for it, the longer it will care for and support us. By nurturing our environment, we're choosing to ensure the good for people across the planet, both now and in future generations.

Caring for the planet often requires small but consistent decisions, such as recycling and purchasing products that are biodegradable or were manufactured using renewable resources. For Dale, it's easy to neglect these choices in favor of what's easiest. He knows what's right, but he often would prefer to buy whatever is cheapest rather than what's best for the environment and to dispose of waste in the way that's quickest rather than what's most responsible.

If we're motivated by compassion, however, we will be pushed to care more for the earth because we care about the people on it. Choose to be intentional about the impact you make on the environment. While caring for our planet is an end unto itself, it's also a way we can express compassion for others.

## Prayer

*God, help me steward the resources you have given me well. Guide me to choose what's best for the earth and the people living on it rather than what's easiest or cheapest. Allow my compassion for people to fuel my desire to preserve your creation so that they can be sustained by it and enjoy it. Amen.*

## Prompt

Spend some time thinking about practical steps you can take to care for the environment. Do you recycle? Do you think critically about the products you purchase, how they were made, who made them, and how you dispose of them? Research and brainstorm how you can live more sustainably with the express purpose of having compassion for others.

# Choose Compassion
# Over Nationalism

*But our citizenship is in heaven. And we eagerly await*
*a Savior from there, the Lord Jesus Christ.*

Philippians 3:20, New International Version

Paul had a unique voice in the early Church because he was a Roman citizen. He was afforded certain rights and comforts that were not available to noncitizens living within the empire. But wherever he went, he never flaunted his superiority over anyone and often gave up his comforts to better serve others.

The church in Philippi had many Roman citizens in its midst, and Paul called them to take the same approach to their citizenship as he did. While they have power through earthly citizenship, they ought not wield that power for personal gain. Instead, they should identify, first and foremost, as citizens of heaven.

There might be times when you have to give up some of your rights as a citizen of the country you live in for the sake of extending compassion globally. That won't always be easy, and it might even be painful for you. In those moments, it's important to remember that you are, first and foremost, a citizen of heaven. Your greatest concern, even over your own nationalism, should be for the good of others.

What would it look like to lay aside your identity as a citizen of a certain country for the sake of ministering to and blessing others. Your country of origin is an important part of your identity. But the greatest shaper of your life is Jesus and the identity He has given you.

In situations in which your identity with your country might get in the way of extending compassion to people of a different culture or ethnicity, it's important to choose compassion over nationalism. There are moments when the countries in which we live don't get it right. As heart-wrenching as that may be, we should see it as an opportunity to show the world the heart of Jesus in spite of the decisions made by world leaders or our given political parties.

You have a greater power than the country you live in. You walk in the power of the Holy Spirit, and he will continue to lead you down the road of compassion.

## Prayer

*Lord, please open my eyes to see the ways in which my worldview is being shaped by my citizenship to a country rather than my citizenship in heaven. I want the lens through which I view my life to be Jesus rather than my early citizenship. I know you have placed me in this country for a reason, and I pray I can use that for your glory. Help me extend compassion over nationalism, and make me aware of that opportunity. Amen.*

## Prompt

This week, challenge yourself to spend less time engaging with the media and more time engaging with scripture. The media's agenda isn't to bring you closer to the heart of Jesus. In fact, it often encourages outrage and anger toward others. Would you commit to trading 10 minutes or more from time spent on media to time spent in the Bible?

# Pray for Other Nations

*I urge you, first of all, to pray for all people. Ask God to help them; intercede on their behalf, and give thanks for them.*

1 Timothy 2:1, New Living Translation

One of the greatest ways to care for someone is to pray for them. That's what Paul told Timothy as he was preparing him to lead the church of Ephesus. This call isn't only for pastors. It's a call to every single person who follows Jesus.

Tamara took a global missions course in college, where the professor gave an assignment that was truly impactful: pray for one country for the entire semester. Each week, she would gather with a group of students and pray for a different aspect of what was happening in that country or for its specific needs. She interceded on behalf of a group of people she'd never met but had quickly learned so much about. To this day, she's never visited that country, but she has a deep heart for it.

There is power in praying on behalf of another person. It takes great compassion to hear about and engage with the challenges someone on the other side of the world is facing—challenges you couldn't even begin to comprehend. Though you are worlds apart, both culturally and geographically, God loves them just as much as he loves you. He sent his Son to die for them just as he did for you.

As you pray for others, your heart will soften toward them, and you will begin to love people you've never met, just as Jesus does. Being intentional about praying for people you've never met displays a great understanding of the heart of God. Your prayers are far more powerful than you may realize.

## Prayer

*Father, I want to have a heart like yours. I want to be able to genuinely love people I've never met and have compassion for them. I want my heart to be for all people and not just the ones I'm currently familiar with. Would you show me who you want me to pray for? Would you place on my heart a specific country or group of people to be intentional about praying for every day? Amen.*

## Prompt

Ask God to place a country in your heart so that you can regularly pray for the people there. Learn more about that country and the specific ways you should pray for them. Set a dedicated time each week to learn about the people there and pray for them. Allow yourself to connect with the struggles and pain of the people for whom you're praying.

# Model Compassion
# to the Next Generation

*One generation commends your works to another; they
tell of your mighty acts.*

Psalm 145:4, New International Version

Compassion is as much a generational mission as it is a
global one. Psalm 145 is a song written by King David in
which he does his best to put words to the immeasurable
goodness of God. He speaks of the Lord's greatness and his
unending compassion for the people he created. Yet it is the
current generation that will share how great God is to the
next generation.

The responsibility of showing the next generation what
it means to be changed by Jesus rests on the current one.
God's work is on display in the lives of this generation of
believers. God's compassionate heart for people of every culture, ethnicity, class, and country is tangibly seen through
the way current believers live.

The next generation is watching, and they're seeing how
this generation displays the compassion of God to people
in other parts of the world. This is a great call, and it might
feel too heavy. But the Spirit will equip you. As you continue
to step into global compassion, the next generation that is
watching you will see the heart of God. It's a privilege that
Jesus would use broken vessels like us to display his glory.
As David says in Psalm 145:3 (New International Version),
*"[God's] greatness no one can fathom."*

You have a role to play in the lives of the next generation.
Part of that role is to display the heart of God in action. His

heart is for every nation and tongue to come to know him as Lord and Savior. This is part of the impact you get to make for the Kingdom of God.

## Prayer

*God, the idea of impacting the next generation seems heroic and far too tall a task. Would you equip me and walk with me as I'm still figuring out how I can be more compassionate to people not in my own country? I want my heart to reflect yours and for the next generation of believers to see you. I don't want them to see me. Rather, I want them to see how you can work through someone broken like me. Amen.*

## Prompt

Write down the names of two or three people who are younger than you whom you would like to bring along on your journey toward growing in global compassion. Be intentional about your conversations with them and find ways to talk about God's care for people. Resist the temptation to feel as though you need to have all the answers. Allow them to be part of your growth process.

# Diversify Your Friend Group

*My dear brothers and sisters, how can you claim to have faith in our glorious Lord Jesus Christ if you favor some people over others?*

James 2:1, New Living Translation

It's completely natural to gravitate toward people who are like you. But James warns us to be aware of that implicit bias and resist it. We're called not to favor certain people (or peoples) over another.

In this passage, James uses the example of favoring rich people over poor people and treating them with greater honor. But the thrust of what he's warning us against is being prejudiced against certain types of people, regardless of what those distinctions might be. The biases we hold about others are often unintentional, so we need to be intentional about rooting them out.

One way you can root out bias in your life is by taking a look at your friend group. Does everyone you consider close to you represent one culture, language, and ethnicity? The body of Christ is diverse in every way you can think of, and our lives should be a reflection of that.

There's great beauty in allowing diversity into your closest circles. It may be a bit uncomfortable. It might feel like a stretch. But there is a richness of life Jesus brings as he unites all of his people. You will have the opportunity to allow your faith to grow and see the love of Jesus through a different lens.

136   PRACTICING CHRISTIAN COMPASSION

Whereas prejudice and bias limit understanding, when you intentionally surround yourself with a variety of God's children, you gain an expanded view of the world. It even expands your view of God.

## Prayer

*Father, thank you for making a world full of diversity. As I search within my own life, would you reveal the places where I have been biased against certain types of people? I want to be open and accepting of my own tendencies and shortcomings. I lay them down at your feet and ask that you would open my heart to embrace change. Please bring people into my life who will help me exemplify the diversity you have created. Amen.*

## Prompt

Think of two people you know who are of a different ethnicity or culture. What are some ways you can develop a deeper relationship with them and allow them into your inner circle? Commit to setting up a time to have lunch or grab a cup of coffee with them. You can start small. Don't feel pressured to try to make them your best friends.

## BENEFITS OF COMPASSION

If you spend much time watching the news, you probably get the distinct impression that the world is a very dark and hostile place. Every day, you hear stories of war, crime, racism, and civil unrest. It's easy to demonize the *other*—the one who looks different from you, who lives in a different region from you, and whose culture is different from yours. You may begin to fear them and see them as a threat to people like you.

The beauty of compassion is that it flips that script. Instead of seeing those people as *other*, you choose, instead, to empathize with them. You learn their story and begin to realize that you have far more in common with them than you originally thought.

And that's when you come to know that the world isn't necessarily a hostile place. It's simply a place that's filled with people who are just like you. People who are broken. People who don't always do what's right. But people who have beauty within them and who need to be cared for.

When you cultivate global compassion, you experience love instead of fear—empathy instead of apathy. You're empowered to see the world from a different point of view and do something to make a change for the better.

# Resources

## Organizations

**AND Campaign** is an organization that seeks to educate and equip Christians to engage in social justice in a way that's grounded in biblical values. Learn more at ANDCampaign.org.

**Charity Water** is an organization seeking to end the global water crisis through the construction of wells. One hundred percent of each donation goes to the work of providing water to those who need it most. Learn more at CharityWater.org.

**Compassion International** is a child sponsorship program that pairs donors with a child. Your monthly donation goes directly toward providing essential resources for that child. Learn more at Compassion.com.

**International Justice Mission** is an organization seeking to end slavery and human trafficking around the world. Learn more at IJM.org.

**Mosaix Global Network** is a parachurch ministry that helps resource local churches and church planters to create more diversity in the local church. Learn more at Mosaix.info.

# Books, Articles, and Websites

*Be the Bridge: Pursuing God's Heart for Racial Reconciliation* by Latasha Morrison offers a practical look at how to step into the work of racial division. Morrison uses biblical principles to help you navigate this difficult topic. This book can be used in a group setting or for your personal growth.

*A Compassionate Call to Counter Culture* by David Platt deals with the current culture issues of our day. It includes topics like racism, same-sex marriage, pornography, and much more. Platt looks at these issues from the perspective of the gospel and encourages readers to respond with compassion and courage.

*The Uneasy Conscience of Modern Fundamentalism* by Carl F. H. Henry argues that the fundamentals of the Christian faith should drive us toward deeper engagement with the culture rather than into withdrawal. Though it was published in 1947, it is just as relevant today as when it was written.

"Cultivate Compassion in Your Kids" is an article by Pastor Matthew Barnett on behalf of a ministry called Focus on the Family. Barnett includes practical steps for you to implement compassion with your family or the children in your life.

*Christianity Today*, christianitytoday.com, is a wonderful place to access articles on daily Christian living. It has a wide range of articles regarding exercising compassion in your life and around the world as laid out in scripture.

# Verse Index

# Acknowledgments

We've always dreamed of writing a book to help others live out their faith in practical ways. We admit that we didn't think it would happen this soon, but God's timing is perfect.

Thank you to Vanessa Putt for your persistence and belief in us as authors. And this project wouldn't have been possible without the kind and thoughtful editing of Andrea Leptinsky.

Individually, Tamara would like to thank Dale for being the best partner to write this book with. You have a way of keeping my feet to the fire and reminding me of the importance of this project in the midst of working full time and changing dirty diapers. I'm so grateful the Lord blessed me with a partner for all things in life.

Likewise, Dale would like to recognize Tamara for being an amazing wife, mom, and co-author who also works a full-time job—all at the same time! Thanks for keeping me encouraged and always reminding me that "we got this."

Together, we want to thank everyone who has been so supportive of us, including (but not limited to) Dawn Sifuentes, Joe and Stacey Monaco, Mike and Joyce Young, and Baldemar and Judy Baldovinos.

# About the Authors

**Dale** and **Tamara Chamberlain** are married authors and speakers who are passionate about loving and serving Jesus together. Through their blog and podcast, they seek to create a space for others to discover the abundant life that Jesus promises us. They each hold a Master of Divinity from Talbot School of Theology. You can connect with Dale and Tamara at HerAndHymn.com.